RockRecipes 2

More Great Food and Photos
From My Newfoundland Kitchen

Barry C. Parsons

WWW.BREAKWATERBOOKS.COM

Breakwater Books is committed to choosing papers and materials for our books that help to protect our environment. To this end, this book is printed on a recycled paper that is certified by the Forest Stewardship Council of Canada.

A CIP catalogue record for this book is available from Library and Archives Canada.

ISBN 978-1-55081-612-9 (bound)

Copyright © 2015 Barry C. Parsons
Reprinted February 2016

We acknowledge the financial support of the Government of Canada and the Government of Newfoundland and Labrador through the Department of Tourism, Culture and Recreation for our publishing activities.

PRINTED AND BOUND IN CANADA.

To

Lynn, for all she does.

Contents

Introduction 6

Chicken 8

Beef, Pork, and Lamb 36

Seafood 60

Quick and Easy Dinners . . 84

Slow-Cooked Sunday. . . . 112

Side Dishes and Soups 138

Brunch 170

Cookies and Bars. 198

Cakes. 226

Dessert 252

Index. 284

If somebody had told me that I would be sitting here writing the introduction to my second cookbook barely six months after the first was released, I would have thought they had taken leave of their senses. It sure has been a busy, eventful year with a lot of firsts: first cookbook, first book-launch party, first book signing, first live on-stage cooking demonstration at the Toronto Convention Centre, even a first live morning television appearance in Halifax.

All of that would have been quite inconceivable to me just a few short years ago, but here indeed I sit, after just completing the majority of the work for this second cookbook. All of this is, of course, due to the great outpouring of support that loyal fans of my blog have shown for the book and the many more folks along the way who were introduced to my work for the first time. It has been a bit of an overwhelming experience I can tell you.

The process of creating my first cookbook made me all the more eager to write a second. I have written and photographed over 1400 recipes in the past eight years on *RockRecipes.com*, so making recipe choices for the first book was quite

difficult. Many popular recipes did not make it into the first book, so it's great to be able to include some of them in a second volume, as well as lots of recipe successes from the past year on my blog. This volume also includes more original recipes developed just for this book, so even the biggest *Rock Recipes* fans are sure to find lots of new cooking and baking ideas.

This book stays true to what my readers consistently tell me they like about *Rock Recipes*—achievable recipes with great taste made from readily available ingredients. I always say that my recipes are "real food for real life," and that's what I firmly believe. I know that approach is what people have responded to, and it's what has provided the success that both my blog and first book have enjoyed. I hope that recipe for success continues with this book and that you find new ideas for bringing family and friends together to enjoy great company with delicious, simple food.

It's no surprise that chicken recipes still continue to be the most searched for on *RockRecipes.com*. Get a good, simple chicken recipe right and it's bound to draw plenty of attention. The recipes chosen here run the gamut from well-established favourites, like Baked General Tso Chicken, to recent hits and late additions, like Honey Dijon Garlic Chicken Breasts. Be sure to check out the Quick and Easy Meals and the Slow-Cooked Sundays sections for even more great chicken dishes sure to please the whole family.

chicken

Honey Dijon Garlic Chicken Breasts 10

Smoked Paprika Chicken *and* Potatoes 12

Oven-Fried Chicken Wings *with* Honey Molasses BBQ Sauce 14

Glazed Sesame Chicken 16

Easy Mango Chicken Curry 18

Barbecue Chicken Chili 20

Baked General Tso Chicken 22

Smoky Chipotle Fried Chicken 24

Crispy Baked Orange Hoisin Chicken 26

Chicken Margherita Cannelloni 28

Curry Chicken Burgers *with* Quick Mango Chutney 30

Orange Five-Spice Broiled Chicken 32

Prosciutto Wrapped Roasted Red Pepper *and* Mozzarella Stuffed Chicken Breasts 34

Honey Dijon Garlic Chicken Breasts

PREP TIME: **10** MINUTES | COOK TIME: **30** MINUTES | SERVES **4**

4 large boneless, skinless **chicken breasts**, about 6 oz each

salt and **pepper** to season

3 tbsp butter

6 cloves garlic, minced

⅓ cup honey

2 tbsp whole-grain Dijon mustard

This recipe came about when I couldn't decide whether to have a honey garlic or honey Dijon chicken for dinner. I decided against deciding and combined the two with a totally delectable result. I love the fact that the chicken breasts are baked at high heat, so they're perfectly cooked in about 30 minutes; that makes this recipe easy to achieve, even as a weekday dinner. I like to preheat the pan as I'm preparing the glaze, which also helps speed things up once the chicken hits the oven. This is a new recipe at our house, but I know it's one we'll make many times. I'll bet when you taste it, you'll say the same.

1. Preheat the oven to 425°F and lightly season the chicken breasts with salt and pepper.

2. Line an 8x8-inch baking pan with aluminum foil. Use a baking pan that is large enough to have a half-inch of space around each chicken breast but no more. Using too large a baking dish can cause the glaze to be too shallow in the pan and burn easily. Place the empty pan in the oven to heat up while you prepare the glaze.

3. To prepare the glaze, melt the butter in a small sauté pan. Add the garlic and cook for only 30-60 seconds to soften it. Do not brown the garlic.

4. Add the honey, Dijon mustard, and a pinch of salt and pepper. Stir well to blend, and simmer over medium heat for 1-2 minutes to begin reducing the glaze.

5. Remove the hot pan from the oven and place the chicken breasts an equal distance apart in the pan. Pour the hot glaze evenly over the chicken.

6. Return the pan to the 425°F oven and bake for 15 minutes. Remove from oven and baste the breasts with the glaze in the bottom of the pan. Return to the oven for an additional 15-20 minutes or until a meat thermometer inserted into the center of the thickest part of the breast reads 170°F.

7. Allow the chicken to rest for 5 minutes before serving.

Smoked Paprika Chicken *and* Potatoes

PREP TIME: **30** MINUTES | COOK TIME: **60** MINUTES | SERVES **4**

SMOKED PAPRIKA CHICKEN

3 lb fresh chicken pieces or
1 whole chicken, halved

3 tbsp olive oil

1½ tbsp smoked paprika

1 tsp granulated garlic

½ tsp kosher salt

½ tsp coarsely ground
black pepper

1 tsp dry thyme

ROASTED POTATOES

2 lb russet potatoes

salt and pepper to season

4–6 tbsp olive oil

½ head garlic cloves, unpeeled

½ tsp smoked paprika (optional)

I certainly write a lot about meal planning, make-ahead shortcuts, and quick and easy meals on *RockRecipes.com*. These are all essentials for getting dinner on the table, while eating real food and, probably most of all, keeping it interesting. It can get pretty hard mustering some dinner enthusiasm from the family if there's always the "same old, same old" meals in your menu rotation. That's why I enjoy making lots of variations of things like roast chicken.

Roast chicken doesn't necessarily come under the banner of a quick and easy meal, but it doesn't have to be an all-day affair either. This fantastically flavourful smoked paprika chicken version is cooked on top of a bed of roasted potatoes in only about 90 minutes for a practically complete meal. I roast two half chickens or chicken pieces on top of the potatoes, which not only provides crispy potatoes as a side dish, but also allows for good air circulation around the meat and helps it to roast quickly and evenly. There's never a morsel left on the platter when this dish gets served up for dinner at our place.

SMOKED PAPRIKA CHICKEN

1. If using a whole chicken, cut it in half by removing the backbone and splitting through the breast bone, or use large chicken pieces.

2. Pat the chicken dry with paper towels.

3. Mix all the remaining ingredients together and rub the mix liberally all over the chicken. Let it marinate in the fridge while you get the potatoes ready, or even overnight if you want to plan ahead.

ROASTED POTATOES

1. Preheat the oven to 400°F. Heat a 9x13-inch roasting pan or dish in the oven at the same time.

2. Peel the potatoes and cut them into 3-inch chunks if they are large.

3. Boil for 5 minutes in salted water before draining all the water off.

4. Return the potatoes to the pot, put the cover back on, and give the pot a few good shakes to rough up the surface of the potatoes. This helps them get crispier. Let them steam off for 5 minutes.

5. Add a pinch of salt and pepper along with the olive oil and garlic cloves and the smoked paprika if you are using it. Toss together well to coat the potatoes in the oil.

6. Working quickly, take the hot pan from the oven and add the contents of the potato pot. The potatoes should sizzle as they hit the pan. This ensures they won't stick. Get them back into the hot oven immediately and cook for 15 minutes.

7. After 15 minutes, turn the potatoes once and place the marinated chicken pieces, skin side up, on top of them. Return the pan to the oven for 45-60 minutes, depending on the size of your chicken pieces, until the chicken is fully cooked. It should be nicely browned and the internal temperature of the largest pieces should be at least 170-175°F on a meat thermometer.

8. Let the chicken rest for 5-10 minutes before serving.

Oven-Fried Chicken Wings
with Honey Molasses BBQ Sauce

PREP TIME: **20** MINUTES | COOK TIME: **1** HOUR | SERVES **3 LBS OF WINGS**

OVEN-FRIED CHICKEN WINGS

3 lb fresh chicken wings

2 eggs

4 tbsp milk

DREDGE MIXTURE

2 cups flour

1 tsp freshly grated nutmeg

½ tsp cayenne pepper

2 tsp salt

1 tsp freshly ground black pepper

1 tbsp dry oregano

1 tsp dry thyme

1 tbsp powdered ginger

1 tsp garlic powder

1½ tsp salt

HONEY MOLASSES BBQ SAUCE

1¾ cups plain tomato sauce

4 tbsp apple-cider vinegar

2 cloves garlic, finely minced

⅓ cup fancy molasses

½ cup honey

1 tsp ground ginger

1 tsp chipotle powder

1 tbsp ground fennel seed

1 tsp freshly ground black pepper

1 tbsp ground dry oregano

½ tsp kosher salt

There are a lot of great chicken wing recipes on *RockRecipes.com*, but this has been one of the most popular right from the beginning. I've often made this same recipe in a deep-fried version as well, but these days I'm finding that, with the right technique, you can easily achieve crunchy, satisfying wings by oven baking.

I sometimes find molasses-based BBQ sauces to be a little too strongly flavoured, so this recipe uses honey as well to maintain the sweetness of the sauce while mellowing the flavour of the molasses.

OVEN-FRIED CHICKEN WINGS

1. Preheat oven to 375°F.

2. Wash the chicken wings and pat dry with paper towels. Trim the tips off and cut the wings into 2 pieces.

3. Whisk together the eggs and milk to make an egg wash and set aside.

4. Blend together all of the ingredients included in the Dredge Mixture. To make sure they are well blended, you can use a food processor if you like.

5. Dip each wing into the flour dredge, then in the egg wash, and back into the flour dredge again. Press each wing firmly into the flour dredge to get good contact then gently shake off any excess.

6. Place on a lightly oiled baking sheet and lightly drizzle or spray the tops with a little more canola oil. Don't crowd the pan. Leave a little space between each wing.

7. Bake for about 45-60 minutes, depending on the size of the wings. Flip the wing pieces halfway through the cooking time. Serve with Honey Molasses BBQ Sauce.

tip > When entertaining guests at one of our "Sips and Nibbles" get-togethers, I often make these a couple hours ahead of time and simply warm them on a wire rack over a cookie sheet at about 375°F for 10 minutes or so when it's time to serve.

HONEY MOLASSES BBQ SAUCE

1. Simply add all of the ingredients to a small saucepan and simmer over medium-low heat.

2. Stir the sauce occasionally and simmer for 20-30 minutes or until the sauce thickens to a consistency similar to ketchup.

Glazed Sesame Chicken

PREP TIME: **10** MINUTES | COOK TIME: **40** MINUTES | SERVES **4–6**

2 to 3 lb chicken parts

3 tbsp soy sauce

2 tbsp water

½ tsp black pepper

½ cup brown sugar

2 tbsp toasted sesame oil

3 tbsp toasted sesame seeds

I really like the extremely simple glaze on this chicken. Using very few ingredients, the glaze relies on the great flavour of toasted sesame oil, one of my favourite additions to any Asian inspired dish.

I'm partial to drumsticks for this recipe because they only take about 40 minutes total time in the oven. Wings would be about the same, so this recipe makes a very welcome addition to any weekday meal plan. Thicker pieces of thigh or breast will take longer, so, as always, have your meat thermometer handy to get a safe internal temperature of 185°F.

1. Preheat oven to 375°F.

2. Wash the chicken parts well and pat dry on paper towels.

3. In a small saucepan, add the soy sauce, water, pepper, brown sugar, and sesame oil.

4. Bring to a rolling boil over medium-low heat until the sauce resembles the consistency of warm honey.

5. Pour the sauce over the chicken parts and toss well.

6. Place the pieces on a parchment-paper lined, aluminum baking sheet. Don't crowd the pieces together; leave an inch or two between them to allow for good heat circulation.

7. Bake for about 35-50 minutes depending upon the size of the chicken pieces. Wings and drumsticks will be faster than thighs and larger breast pieces.

8. Turn the pieces every 10 minutes and spoon a little of the glaze/sauce from the bowl each time you turn them.

9. Let the chicken rest for 5 minutes on the pan before serving with a generous sprinkle of the toasted sesame seeds.

tips for glazing chicken
> Many people have difficulties with sweet glazes for chicken. Here are some tips to help alleviate the problems:

1. Make sure you use good quality aluminum bakeware. Cheaper quality alloy bakeware, the kind that turns dark brown or black after lots of use, is often the problem. Some of those pans carry the heat far too quickly for many recipes, especially baking. Aluminum buffers the heat and distributes it more evenly and slowly.

2. Parchment paper is a great help. The layer of paper acts as an additional buffer, and I've found the sugars in glazes will cook for longer without burning on parchment paper.

3. Don't start with a glaze that's too thick, on the thinner side is better. Turn and re-glaze the chicken often. This way the chicken builds up the glaze more slowly and the pan gets a minute or two to rest from the direct heat.

MARINATED GRILLED CHICKEN

6 boneless, skinless chicken breasts (or a dozen boneless, skinless chicken thighs)

3 tbsp tandoori masala
(you can substitute garam masala)

3 tbsp lime juice

½ tsp black pepper

½ tsp salt

3 tbsp peanut oil

MANGO CURRY

1 large red onion, finely chopped

4 cloves garlic, minced

4 tbsp peanut oil

2 tsp garam masala

1 tsp tandoori masala

1 tsp turmeric

½ tsp cinnamon

½ tsp ground cumin

¼ tsp ground cloves

½ tsp ground cardamom

1 tbsp chili powder

1 tsp ground fennel seeds

1 tsp ground coriander seeds

½ tsp red curry powder

1 tbsp ground fenugreek leaves (methi)

2 tbsp yellow curry powder

3 tbsp lemon juice

3 tbsp brown sugar

2 or 3 large ripe mangoes, peeled, pitted, and pureed

2 cups coconut milk

2 tbsp freshly grated ginger root

1 cup water (or chicken stock)

1 tsp salt

1 tsp black pepper

1 large red bell pepper, grilled and diced

1 large mango, diced

3 tbsp butter

Easy Mango Chicken Curry

PREP TIME: 10 MINUTES + 1 HOUR MARINATING TIME
COOK TIME: 40 MINUTES | SERVES 6–8

Like so many of the recipes I develop, this one borrows elements from several recipes I've tried to ultimately make a dish that suits my own taste. I'd call this recipe one of the most successful results from taking that approach.

Pureed mangoes form the base of the sauce upon which the complex flavours and textures get built. Exotically spicy, lightly sweet with an acidic touch, and with added smokiness from the grilled chicken—this really is a well-balanced, spicy, sweet flavour combination that is absolutely delicious served over plain steamed rice or with your favourite fresh Naan. It's also a great opportunity to head to the bulk store to restock your spices if you haven't done so in a while. It will be well worth the trip.

MARINATED GRILLED CHICKEN

1. Place the chicken breasts or thighs into a large Ziploc bag.

2. Mix together the 3 tbsp tandoori masala (or garam masala), lime juice, black pepper, salt, and 3 tbsp peanut oil. Pour over the chicken, making sure it's well coated before marinating in the fridge for about an hour.

3. Completely cook the chicken breasts on a gas or charcoal grill and set aside to rest for a few minutes before cutting the chicken into about 1-inch cubes.

Alternatively, you can cook the chicken under the broiler on a high setting or 425°F for just a few minutes per side. You can also grill the red bell pepper, which gets added at the end, while cooking the chicken.

MANGO CURRY

1. In a large saucepan or Dutch oven over medium heat, sauté together the onions, garlic, and the 4 tbsp peanut oil for just a couple of minutes until the onions begin to soften. Add all of the spices: garam masala, tandoori masala, turmeric, cinnamon, cumin, cloves, cardamom, chili powder, ground fennel seeds, coriander seeds, red curry powder, fenugreek powder, and yellow curry powder. Cook together in the onions for a couple of minutes to release their flavours.

2. Add the lemon juice, brown sugar, pureed mangoes, coconut milk, grated ginger root, water, salt, and pepper. Simmer together over low heat for about 25-30 minutes, stirring occasionally.

3. Add the diced chicken to the sauce and simmer for an additional 5 minutes.

4. Add the grilled pepper, diced mango, and butter and simmer for 10 minutes more, to warm through the mango and peppers.

Barbecue Chicken Chili

PREP TIME: **25** MINUTES | COOK TIME: **35** MINUTES | SERVES **6–8**

DRY RUB

½ tsp cumin

1 tbsp smoked paprika

½ tsp garlic powder

½ tsp onion powder

1 tbsp chili powder

1 tsp kosher salt

½ tsp black pepper

CHILI

2½–3 lb boneless, skinless chicken thighs or breasts

3 ears sweet corn, grilled

1 large grilled bell pepper, diced small

4 cloves garlic, minced

1 medium red onion, finely diced

3 tbsp olive oil

3½ cups diced tomatoes (canned or fresh)

2½ cups plain tomato sauce

3 tbsp molasses

1 cup grated zucchini (optional, squeeze to remove excess liquid)

2 cups canned kidney beans (drained and rinsed)

This recipe takes a classic comfort-food meal and gives it a fresh summertime twist: bright, light, and totally delicious. When summer-fresh tomatoes, corn, and zucchini are plentiful, this is a tasty way to use them all in a seasonal meal. In this recipe, the dry rub is the only seasoning the chili needs to keep it light, fresh tasting, and still well-seasoned.

Grilling the chicken, corn, and peppers adds plenty of smoky flavour while keeping the overall taste very fresh. The crunchy kernels of sweet corn add delectable little bursts of flavour. In winter, you can grill the marinated chicken under the broiler and use canned tomatoes and even frozen corn to replicate some delicious summer flavour when it is most needed.

---

1. Mix all of the ingredients in the Dry Rub together well. Coat the chicken with the dry rub, cover, and place in the fridge for a couple of hours or overnight.

2. Grill the chicken, corn, and peppers. Dice the chicken and peppers into bite-sized pieces and remove the corn kernels from the cob.

3. In a Dutch oven or large saucepan, sauté the garlic and onions in the olive oil until the onions begin to soften.

4. Add the tomatoes, tomato sauce, molasses, sweet corn, grilled pepper, grated zucchini (optional), and kidney beans.

5. Simmer for about 20 minutes before adding the grilled chicken and simmering for an additional 15 minutes.

tip > If you like, you can even grill the chicken, corn, and peppers the day before, especially if you are grilling anyway, and get a big jump on the next day's dinner.

Baked General Tso Chicken

PREP TIME: **20** MINUTES | COOK TIME: **20** MINUTES | SERVES **4–6**

BAKED CHICKEN

1 cup flour

½ tsp black pepper

¼ tsp cayenne pepper

3 tbsp ground ginger

1 tsp salt

2–3 lb boneless chicken thighs or breasts, cut in strips

1 egg + 2 tbsp water whisked together to make an egg wash

GENERAL TSO SAUCE

4 tbsp soy sauce

4 tbsp rice wine vinegar (white wine vinegar is fine in a pinch)

¼ cup water

2 tbsp toasted sesame oil

2 tsp paprika

2 tbsp crushed chili paste, or to taste (or 1 tsp chili flakes)

1 tsp salt

2 tsp cornstarch

3 cloves garlic, minced

3 tbsp freshly grated ginger

1 cup sugar

¼ cup water

This recipe has to be called a *Rock Recipes* all-star. I first posted it to my blog early in 2009, and it has consistently maintained a place in our top ten most viewed recipes. It's no surprise, really. The simple recipe shows how to make one of the most popular Chinese take-out dishes of all time and with less fat than the deep-fried version. The recipe has received tons of great reviews from readers who have tried it, and many declare it's even better than any restaurant version they've ever tasted.

BAKED CHICKEN

1. Preheat oven to 425° F.

2. Combine the flour, black pepper, cayenne pepper, ground ginger, and salt.

3. Season the chicken pieces with salt and pepper then dip them in the egg wash before dredging them in the flour mixture to completely coat them on all sides.

4. Place on a lightly oiled baking sheet and lightly drizzle over the tops with a little more olive oil.

5. Bake for about 20 minutes. Flip the pieces halfway through the cooking time.

GENERAL TSO SAUCE

1. While the chicken is baking, prepare your sauce. Don't walk away from this sauce; it gets very hot when making the caramel base and can burn easily, so pay careful attention while cooking.

2. In a small bowl, mix together the soy sauce, rice wine vinegar, ¼ cup water, toasted sesame oil, paprika, chili paste, salt, cornstarch, minced garlic, and grated ginger. Set this mixture aside.

3. In a medium saucepan or wok, boil together the sugar and ¼ cup of water.

4. Boil this over medium heat, watching constantly until the caramel starts to turn a light amber colour and you can begin to smell the caramel. Do not stir. When it reaches this stage, give the other ingredients in the bowl a quick stir to make sure the cornstarch is dissolved then add it all at once to the hot caramel. (Careful: This mixture is very hot and will release a lot of steam at this point!)

5. Be vigilant at this stage because this sauce can foam up considerably for a few seconds, and it is very hot. Simmer for only a few minutes then remove from the heat and allow to cool down slightly.

6. Toss the sauce with the cooked chicken pieces and serve over plain steamed rice or Chinese noodles.

Smoky Chipotle Fried Chicken

PREP TIME: **20** MINUTES + BRINING TIME | COOK TIME: **40** MINUTES | SERVES **4**

BRINING LIQUID

2 quarts (litres) of **water**

¼ cup **kosher salt**

¼ cup **brown sugar**

2 tbsp **honey** or **maple syrup**

3 tbsp **black peppercorns**

8 **cloves garlic**, thinly sliced

1 **large onion**, thinly sliced

½ cup **Tabasco sauce** (add more if you like)

1 **large chicken**, about 3½ to 4 lb

FLOUR AND SPICE DREDGE

1½ cups **all-purpose flour**

1 tsp **kosher salt**

1 tsp **freshly ground black pepper**

3 heaping tbsp **smoked paprika**

2 heaping tbsp **chipotle powder**

SMOKY CHIPOTLE FRIED CHICKEN

vegetable oil for frying

½ cup **butter** for frying

I have a particular love for smoky spices, so I chose a combination of smoked paprika and chipotle powder to easily but intensely flavour the crust on this new version of fried chicken. I knew that would work well, but what about flavouring the meat under that crispy crust? The answer was to brine the chicken pieces overnight or longer.

Brining poultry is something you just must try if you never have. It means simply soaking the meat in a seasoning solution for a period of time. The process adds great flavour and extra juiciness throughout the meat, making it succulent and perfect.

This Smoky Chipotle Fried Chicken is seriously the best fried-chicken recipe I've ever tried, and brining the chicken makes it super tender, juicy, and perfectly seasoned throughout.

---

1. Prepare the Brining Liquid by adding the water, kosher salt, brown sugar, and honey to a large plastic or glass bowl. Stir until the salt and sugar are dissolved then add the peppercorns, garlic, onion, and Tabasco sauce.

2. Drop the chicken pieces into the brining liquid, cover, and refrigerate for 24 to 48 hours. If you need to add a little more water to completely cover the chicken, that's not a problem.

3. After 24-48 hours, remove the chicken from the brine mixture. Pat dry with paper towels.

4. To make the Flour and Spice Dredge, simply toss the flour, salt, pepper, smoked paprika, and chipotle powder together until completely blended.

5. Add the brined chicken pieces to the flour dredge. Toss well and press the chicken pieces into the flour dredge with your palms to get good contact with the meat.

6. Let stand for 10 minutes, then toss again and press down with your palms again. This ensures a good crust on the chicken.

7. Now it's time to warm up your oil and butter. In a 12-inch cast-iron skillet, heat 1 inch canola or corn oil with ½ cup real dairy butter until it reaches 350°F. Just below medium heat works well on my stove, but use a thermometer to be sure. A cast-iron skillet is best for fried chicken. Be extra careful to regulate the heat properly if using anything other than cast iron. Even cooking is essential.

8. Drop the dredged chicken pieces into the hot oil/butter mix and cook for approximately 35-40 minutes, depending on the size of your chicken pieces, turning at least once halfway through the cooking time. I start with the dark meat pieces and add the breasts about 10-15 minutes into the cooking time because these will cook faster. I always use my meat thermometer to ensure that the largest pieces have reached an internal temperature of 175°F, which is perfect for fried chicken. The chicken should be a beautiful golden brown when it comes out of the oil. Let it rest on a wire rack to drain for 10 minutes before serving.

Crispy Baked Orange Hoisin Chicken

PREP TIME: 20 MINUTES | **COOK TIME: 20 MINUTES** | **SERVES 4–6**

This baked version of orange hoisin chicken certainly does not fall short on flavour. It takes mere minutes to bake the chicken to a crispy golden brown in a hot oven and then toss it in a delicious, easy-to-make orange hoisin sauce which you can prepare while the chicken is in the oven.

It's important to heat the pan in the oven first to ensure the chicken gets crispy in the short cooking time. This recipe is terrific served over Chinese noodles or rice for a delicious meal in 30 minutes. Hey, it takes the delivery guy longer than that to make it to your front door.

CRISPY BAKED CHICKEN

1 cup flour

½ tsp black pepper

¼ tsp cayenne pepper

1 tbsp ground ginger

½ tsp ground nutmeg

1 tsp salt

4 large boneless, skinless chicken breasts cut in thick strips

1 egg + 2 tbsp water whisked together to make an egg wash

ORANGE HOISIN SAUCE

3 tbsp peanut oil

3 cloves garlic, minced

2 cups orange juice

½ cup hoisin sauce

4 tbsp rice wine or Chinese cooking wine

3 tbsp rice wine vinegar (or apple cider vinegar in a pinch)

6 tbsp brown sugar

2 tsp chili paste (optional or to taste or use chili flakes to taste)

4 tsp soya sauce

2 tsp toasted sesame oil

cornstarch slurry (2 tsp cornstarch and ¼ cup cold water)

1 red bell pepper, diced

1 cup sliced button mushrooms (optional)

1 cup steamed snow peas

CRISPY BAKED CHICKEN

1. Preheat a baking pan in a 425°F oven.

2. Combine the flour, pepper, cayenne pepper, ground ginger, nutmeg, and salt.

3. Dredge the chicken pieces in the flour mixture, then in the egg wash, then again in the flour mixture.

4. Place on a lightly oiled baking sheet and lightly drizzle over the tops with a little more peanut oil.

5. Bake for about 20 minutes. Flip the pieces halfway through the cooking time.

6. While the chicken is baking, prepare your sauce.

ORANGE HOISIN SAUCE

1. Heat peanut oil in a wok over medium-high heat.

2. Quickly add the garlic and stir fry for only about a minute.

3. Add the orange juice and simmer to reduce the volume by half.

4. Add the hoisin sauce, rice wine, vinegar, brown sugar, chili paste, soy sauce, and toasted sesame oil.

5. Bring to a boil and thicken with a cornstarch slurry. Let simmer for 1 minute, stirring constantly.

6. Toss in the baked chicken pieces, diced pepper, mushrooms, and snow peas. Simmer for only a minute or two more, just to warm through the vegetables.

7. Serve over steamed rice or noodles.

Chicken Margherita Cannelloni

PREP TIME: **30** MINUTES | COOK TIME: **40** MINUTES | SERVES **4**

TOMATO SAUCE

4 cloves garlic, minced

6 tbsp olive oil

8–10 large ripe tomatoes, diced

1 tbsp brown sugar

½ tsp crushed-chili sauce or chili flakes

salt and pepper to season

6 tbsp balsamic vinegar

CANNELLONI FILLING

4 large boneless, skinless chicken breasts, diced small

2 cloves garlic, minced

3 tbsp olive oil

salt and pepper to season

3 tbsp chopped fresh basil

2 cups ricotta cheese

½ tsp nutmeg

2 egg yolks

3 tbsp freshly grated Parmesan cheese

CANNELLONI

8 fresh lasagna sheets or cannelloni tubes

about a dozen basil leaves

12 oz grated mozzarella cheese

Our family loves a good baked pasta dish, and this is one of our favourites: not just because of all that delicious cheesy goodness on top, but because it's so easy to prepare. The few simple ingredients provide the bright, fresh, classic Margherita flavour combination of tomato, basil, and mozzarella. No canned tomatoes here, the simple sauce is made from fresh tomatoes and garlic quickly sautéed together in a pan. The chicken is also quickly stir fried then mixed with some creamy ricotta cheese and basil to create the rich filling for the cannelloni—a perfect baked pasta meal, especially when company's coming.

TOMATO SAUCE

1. Sauté the garlic in the olive oil over medium heat for just a minute before adding the tomatoes, brown sugar, chili sauce, salt, and pepper.

2. Continue to cook until the tomatoes soften and the compote reduces to a chunky jam-like consistency. Add the balsamic vinegar and simmer for a final minute or two.

CANNELLONI FILLING

1. Season the diced chicken with salt and pepper then stir fry quickly with the garlic and olive oil for just a few minutes over high heat. Do not overcook: the chicken will be going back into the oven. If you overcook it at this stage, the chicken will be very dry after baking.

2. Set aside to cool for 10 or 15 minutes then add the basil, ricotta, nutmeg, egg yolks, and Parmesan cheese.

CANNELLONI

1. Preheat oven to 350°F.

2. If your lasagna sheets are very large, you can cut them in half. Lasagna sheets of about 6x6 inches is about right, but you can make almost any size work. If the sheets are too stiff, just soak them in warm water for a few minutes until they soften sufficiently to roll.

3. You will need two 8x8-inch baking dishes or one large baking dish of the equivalent size. Spoon a thin layer of the sauce to cover the bottom of the pan/s.

4. Spoon ⅛ of the filling onto each lasagna sheet and gently roll the sheet up into a tube about an inch thick. I find spooning the filling onto the center of the sheet and then rolling works best. As you roll, the filling disperses throughout the pasta tube you are forming.

5. Place the cannelloni in the pan a half inch apart and cover with the remaining sauce, a layer of basil leaves, and then sprinkle on the grated mozzarella evenly. Bake for about 40 minutes until the sauce bubbles and the cheese is melted and begins to brown.

4 large boneless, skinless chicken breasts, diced very small

2 tsp curry powder

1 tsp sea salt

1 tsp freshly ground black pepper

½ tsp Chinese five-spice powder

¾ cup finely diced red bell pepper

2 tbsp extra virgin olive oil (plus a little more for frying)

3 cloves garlic, finely minced

6 burger buns

QUICK MANGO CHUTNEY

1 small red onion, chopped

2 cloves garlic, minced

1½ tbsp olive oil

2 cups diced ripe mangoes

1 tbsp fresh grated ginger root

2 tbsp brown sugar

2 tbsp honey

2 tbsp lemon juice

2 tbsp apple juice

¼ tsp salt

½ tsp pepper

¼ tsp ground cardamom

¼ tsp nutmeg

½ tsp cinnamon

1 tsp garam masala

½ tsp turmeric

¼ tsp chili flakes (optional) or red curry paste/powder to taste

Curry Chicken Burgers *with* Quick Mango Chutney

PREP TIME: 30 MINUTES | COOK TIME: 10 MINUTES
SERVES 6

Now this isn't your everyday chicken burger, but that doesn't mean you couldn't have it any day of the week when a bold flavour break might be most appreciated. I'm not a big fan of making chicken burgers from ground chicken; often the grind is too fine, there's too much fat added, or it's difficult to find "breast only" ground chicken at the supermarket. My solution? I simply take boneless, skinless chicken breasts and dice them very small to form my own rough-grind version of ground chicken. The texture is much meatier with plenty of spicy flavour enhancers inside the mix. It's a technique worth exploring on your own using other flavour combinations to create your new favourite chicken burger.

CHICKEN BURGER

1. Toss all of the burger ingredients together in a glass bowl. You can cover this mixture with plastic wrap and store in the fridge for an hour or two or even overnight in advance of cooking it, which lets the spices penetrate the chicken, but it's perfectly fine to use right away of you don't have the time.

2. Heat a couple of tablespoons of olive oil in a non-stick frying pan over medium heat.

3. Divide the chicken mixture into 6 portions and form each portion into a burger patty. Fry for about 4-5 minutes on each side until fully cooked.

4. Serve the curry chicken patties on toasted buns with the Quick Mango Chutney.

QUICK MANGO CHUTNEY

1. Begin by sautéing together the red onion, garlic, and olive oil in a small pot for a few minutes until softened.

2. Add all the remaining chutney ingredients and simmer together very gently for about 15-20 minutes on medium-low heat, stirring occasionally, until the mixture thickens and resembles a thick chunky jam.

Orange Five-Spice Broiled Chicken

PREP TIME: **10** MINUTES | COOK TIME: **40** MINUTES | SERVES **4–6**

People familiar with my first *Rock Recipes* cookbook will likely recognize this recipe as a variation of the Broiled Lemon Chicken that appears in that volume. I've grown to appreciate easy broiled chicken recipes even more since I published that first book, and even though the recipe is remarkably similar in method, the orange and fragrant five-spice powder provide a completely unique flavour of its own.

1 whole chicken, cut in pieces (or about 3 lb chicken pieces)

3 tbsp olive oil

½ tsp salt

½ tsp freshly ground black pepper

1 tsp Chinese five-spice powder

½ tsp dried thyme or 1 tsp fresh chopped thyme

juice of 2 large or 3 small oranges (reserve the peels for the roasting pan)

1. Wash your chicken pieces well and pat dry with paper towels.

2. Add the chicken pieces to a large shallow pan. It is very important not to crowd the chicken pieces in the pan. They should not touch each other at all and should have at least a half-inch of space between the pieces for good heat circulation and even browning. If necessary, use 2 smaller pans in order not to crowd the pieces together.

3. To the pan add the olive oil, salt, pepper, Chinese five-spice powder, thyme, and orange juice.

4. Toss together well, massaging the chicken pieces well with the orange juice, oil, and seasonings.

5. Spread out the pieces in the pan.

6. Add the orange peel pieces to the pan as well; the roasted orange pieces add extra flavour to the pan drippings.

7. If your broiler is temperature controlled, I would set it at about 400-425°F. But because individual broilers vary greatly, you will have to use some judgment in the cooking method and time to suit your individual broiler. I broiled this chicken on high but kept the pan on the second lowest rack from the bottom. Watch the chicken carefully so it doesn't brown too quickly. If it does start to brown too quickly, lower the rack even further or, if possible, turn the temperature down on your broiler.

8. It is important to turn the chicken several times during the broiling time. I turned the pieces about 4 times during the 35-40 minute cooking time.

9. Use a meat thermometer to take a reading from the center of the largest pieces of chicken, and when the internal temperature reaches 170°F, remove the pieces from the oven and let rest for 5 minutes before serving.

10. Skim the excess fat from the pan drippings and serve over the chicken.

Prosciutto Wrapped Roasted Red Pepper *and* Mozzarella Stuffed Chicken Breasts

PREP TIME: **30** MINUTES | COOK TIME: **30–60** MINUTES | SERVES **4**

Originally appearing on my blog as a Valentine's Day suggestion, this dish is a delicious choice for a romantic dinner for two. The rest of the year, it's ideal to prepare ahead of time as the main course at a dinner party or special family meal; just pop the prepared breast into the oven when your guests arrive and serve with roasted potatoes and steamed vegetables.

The stuffed, wrapped chicken is quite simple to put together and goes refreshingly well with the easy to prepare olive tapenade. If olives are not your thing, you could very easily serve it with some of your favourite marinara sauce and pasta instead.

PROSCIUTTO WRAPPED ROASTED RED PEPPER AND MOZZARELLA STUFFED CHICKEN BREASTS

4 extra-large, boneless, skinless chicken breasts (butterfly cut or pounded to ¼-inch thickness)

4 oz mozzarella cheese, cut in 4 sticks

2 small red bell peppers, roasted

6-8 oz thinly sliced prosciutto

OLIVE TAPENADE

1 cup Kalamata olives, pitted

6 tbsp olive oil

4 tbsp grated Parmesan cheese

1 tbsp capers

pinch black pepper

pinch brown sugar

2 tbsp lemon juice

PROSCIUTTO WRAPPED ROASTED RED PEPPER AND MOZZARELLA STUFFED CHICKEN BREASTS

1. Preheat oven to 350°F.

2. Place chicken pieces on a cutting board and pound to ¼-inch thickness.

3. Wrap each stick of mozzarella with half a roasted red bell pepper and place in the center of each chicken breast.

4. Roll the chicken breast around the red bell pepper.

5. Wrap the chicken breast entirely in thin slices of prosciutto.

6. Place the prepared breasts, fold side down, on a parchment-lined baking sheet and bake for about 1 hour or until the internal temperature of the breasts reaches 175-185°F on a meat thermometer.

7. Let the meat rest for 5-10 minutes before serving. Serve with olive tapenade (or marinara sauce).

OLIVE TAPENADE

1. Simply pulse together all the ingredients in a food processor until well-blended but not completely smooth.

If you're in a chicken rut, the choices offered here are sure to break you out of it with ease. This eclectic mix of recipes takes you from comfort-food classics like Salisbury steak to boredom-busting bold curry flavours and even a spicy peanut butter and bacon burger that really surprises. These dishes will help you with everything: from breezing through weekday suppers to impressing your friends at your next dinner party.

beef, pork, and lamb

Salisbury Steak *with* Mushroom Gravy 38

Curry Pork Chops *with* Easy Plum Chutney 40

Meatloaf *with* Sweet Onion Glaze 42

Peanut Butter Sriracha Bacon Cheeseburger 44

Baked Parmesan Panko Pork Chops *with* Quick Puttanesca Sauce 46

Pan-Seared Pork Chops *with* Dijon Butter Sauce 48

The Best Bolognese Sauce 50

Chicken Fried Pork Chops 52

Garlic and Five-Spice Grilled Steak 54

Souvlaki Roast Pork Loin *with* Lemon Oregano Tzatziki 56

Parmesan Panko Crusted Rack of Lamb 58

Salisbury Steak *with* Mushroom Gravy

PREP TIME: 15 MINUTES | **COOK TIME: 1** HOUR **15** MINUTES | SERVES **4–6**

STEAK PATTIES

3 slices day-old white bread

½ cup milk

2½ lb lean ground beef

¼ tsp ground nutmeg

½ tsp dry thyme

pinch of salt and pepper to season

canola oil for frying

MUSHROOM GRAVY

6 tbsp butter

1 cup sliced, fresh button mushrooms

1 small red onion, finely diced

3 cloves garlic, minced

3 cups low-sodium or salt-free beef stock, heated to almost boiling

3 tbsp flour

3 tbsp Worcestershire Sauce

pinch salt and pepper

My son, Noah, asked me one day, "What exactly is Salisbury steak anyway? Is it even steak?" He'd only ever heard of it and never tried it. I explained as best I could about this throwback to the 70s TV dinner, describing it as sort of "more like meatloaf patties cooked in gravy and served with mashed potatoes." Suddenly it didn't sound so bad at all; it just sounded like a good home-cooked dinner. Taking cues from my meatloaf recipe and some simple mushroom gravy, I set out to revisit the 70s. It was worth the trip. Maybe I should revisit some other out-of-fashion meals because the whole family thought this Salisbury steak was excellent, and we've served it several times since, proving that good home cooking never goes out of style.

1. Pull the bread apart with your fingers into large breadcrumbs. Pour the milk over the breadcrumbs and let stand for 5 minutes and then gently combine the soaked crumbs with the ground beef, nutmeg, thyme, salt, and pepper. Form into 8 oval-shaped patties.

2. Add a little canola oil to a hot cast-iron pan and brown the patties well on both sides, about 2-3 minutes per side on medium-high heat. Remove the browned patties and add them to a covered casserole dish or small covered roasting pan.

3. To make the Mushroom Gravy, drain any excess fat from the cast-iron pan, add the 3 tbsp butter and brown the mushrooms for a few minutes. Add those to the steak patties in the casserole dish.

4. Add the onions and garlic to the cast-iron pan, reduce the heat to medium, and cook until the onions have softened. Add to the casserole dish along with the steak patties and mushrooms.

5. Preheat oven to 325°F.

6. Heat the beef stock to almost boiling. Cook the flour and 3 tbsp of butter together in the cast-iron pan over medium-low heat until foamy, about 2 minutes. Slowly pour in the hot stock and, whisking constantly, add the Worcestershire sauce, salt, and pepper. This will create a thin gravy which is then poured over everything else in the casserole dish or roasting pan. Cover and cook in the oven for about 1 hour. Serve with mashed potatoes and steamed vegetables.

Curry Pork Chops *with* Easy Plum Chutney

PREP TIME: **20** MINUTES + MARINATING TIME | COOK TIME: **20** MINUTES | SERVES **4**

CURRY PORK CHOPS

4 boneless center-loin pork chops

½ tsp kosher salt

½ tsp black pepper

2 tsp garam masala

2 tsp yellow curry powder

2 tbsp peanut oil

EASY PLUM CHUTNEY

1 small red onion, chopped

3 cloves garlic, minced

3 tbsp olive oil

4 cups diced ripe plums

2 tbsp fresh grated ginger root

¼ cup brown sugar

¼ cup honey

¼ cup lemon juice

¼ cup apple juice

½ tsp salt

1 tsp pepper

½ tsp ground cardamom

½ tsp nutmeg

½ tsp cinnamon

2 tsp garam masala

½ tsp turmeric

¼ tsp chili flakes (optional) or red curry paste/powder to taste

These chops need only be marinated for an hour or so, but if you want to let them sit overnight to pick up maximum flavour, that's perfectly fine too. That will give you a head start on this beautifully seasoned pork recipe that's made even better with the sweet and sour, easy plum chutney.

I've used yellow plums here because they were in season at the time, but the recipe can use any plums you like. Other stone fruits like nectarines, peaches, or apricots can also be used in this recipe, but if they are particularly sweet then I'd suggest using half the brown sugar and honey, then adjust the amount by adding a little more at a time and tasting the chutney as it cooks. This will allow you to get the balance just right to suit your own taste.

CURRY PORK CHOPS

1. Clean and pat the pork chops dry.

2. Mix the remaining 5 ingredients to form a marinade and rub it all over the pork chops and place in a Ziploc bag in the fridge for an hour or two or overnight.

3. Grill the pork chops until fully cooked. (You can also pan fry or broil them if you prefer.) I use a meat thermometer to cook them to an internal temperature of 150°F. The residual heat should carry them over to 160°F as they rest.

4. Let the chops rest for 5 minutes before serving with the plum chutney.

EASY PLUM CHUTNEY

1. Begin by sautéing together the red onion, garlic, and olive oil in a small pot for a few minutes until softened.

2. Add all the remaining chutney ingredients and simmer together gently for about 20-30 minutes until the mixture thickens and resembles a thick chunky jam.

3. Serve over the grilled pork chops.

Meatloaf *with* Sweet Onion Glaze

PREP TIME: **30** MINUTES | COOK TIME: **1** HOUR **10** MINUTES | SERVES **6**

MEATLOAF

3 cloves garlic, finely chopped

1 medium red onion, finely diced

2 tbsp olive oil

1 cup bread crumbs

3 oz milk

1½ lb lean ground beef

½ cup finely shredded Parmesan cheese

1 tsp ground black pepper

1 tsp dried thyme

1 tsp dried oregano

½ tsp nutmeg

1 tbsp smoked paprika (optional)

1 egg, beaten

SWEET ONION GLAZE

1 small onion, julienned

3 cloves garlic, minced

3 tbsp olive oil

1 cup plain tomato sauce

½ cup brown sugar

2 tbsp balsamic vinegar

½ tsp black pepper

½ tsp salt

4 tbsp hot sauce (more or less to taste)

4 tbsp Worcestershire sauce

1 tbsp dry mustard powder

1 tsp ground ginger

A good, old-fashioned, homemade meatloaf recipe is hard to beat, and everyone needs a good standard version in their comfort-food repertoire. This has been my standard recipe for at least the last 25 years, but with a little recent updating (a great recipe is always an evolving thing). This meatloaf version stays moist and juicy and gets a major flavour boost from a tangy, sweet onion glaze. Some mixed vegetables and mashed potatoes is all it takes to complete one of the best comfort food meals ever.

MEATLOAF

1. Preheat oven to 375°F.

2. Sauté the garlic and red onion in the olive oil only until softened but not browned.

3. Soak the breadcrumbs in the milk for a few minutes before adding to the ground beef.

4. Mix together the Parmesan cheese, pepper, thyme, oregano, nutmeg, and paprika. Mixing these together first helps to distribute the seasoning evenly through the meatloaf.

5. Add to the ground beef and breadcrumb mixture along with the beaten egg.

6. Combine all well and press into a medium- to large-sized loaf pan. It's a good idea to use a loaf pan that's a little larger than the amount of meatloaf mixture to allow for the addition of the glaze later. The pan I use is perfect. It gets filled to about ½ inch from the top rim.

7. Bake for about 40 minutes.

8. Drain excess fat from the loaf pan and add the sweet onion glaze.

9. Return to oven for an additional 30-45 minutes. Drain excess fat again before serving.

tip > Leftovers can be used for meatloaf sandwiches on toasted crusty bread or, as we often do at our house, as paninis with the addition of some mozzarella or provolone cheese.

SWEET ONION GLAZE

1. In a small saucepan sauté the onion, garlic, and olive oil for about 3 minutes until the onions soften but do not brown.

2. Add the remaining ingredients and simmer slowly for about 20 minutes, stirring occasionally.

Peanut Butter Sriracha Bacon Cheeseburger

PREP TIME: **20** MINUTES | COOK TIME: **10** MINUTES | SERVES **4**

SMOKY SRIRACHA MAYO

½ cup olive-oil mayo

2 tbsp sriracha sauce

1 tsp smoked paprika

BACON BLANKETS

12 strips of bacon, cut in half

SRIRCHA BURGERS

1½ lb medium or lean ground beef

3 tbsp sriracha sauce

6 oz thinly sliced aged cheddar cheese

4 toasted burger buns

4 heaping tbsp of smooth peanut butter

crisp lettuce

sliced tomato

4 heaping tsp sweet green relish

Although I'd seen it many times on menus and food shows, I resisted trying peanut butter on a burger for a very long time. While I was on a short promotional tour for my first cookbook, however, peanut butter appeared on a burger menu once again, and this time I absolutely fell in love. I just had to create my own take on this idea and quickly came up with a recipe that combines sweet, salty, smoky, and spicy flavours in a taste explosion of a burger. There's really nothing like it!

SMOKY SRIRACHA MAYO

1. Simply stir the mayo, sriracha sauce, and smoked paprika together, set aside for later.

BACON BLANKETS

1. Cut the bacon strips in half and weave them into bacon blankets. Fry them until crisp and hold in a warm oven, 150°F, until needed.

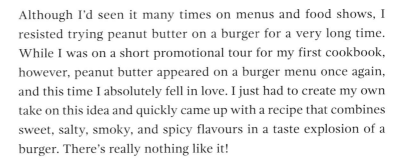

tip > My favourite way to add bacon to a burger is to make a mini bacon blanket. It's simple to do. Just take 3 strips of bacon, cut them in half, and weave them into a square. Fry them in a cast-iron pan, preferably over medium heat, and with a weight on them to keep them flat. An aluminum foil-wrapped brick works well! The bacon blanket is the perfect size for the burger, ensures that there's bacon in every bite, and prevents strips of bacon from falling off onto your plate. A mini bacon blanket is perfect for any burger!

SRIRACHA BURGERS

1. Mix the ground beef with the sriracha sauce and form into four 6-oz patties. I like to pat them out to about a half-inch thickness to allow for shrinking while cooking.

2. Fry on a cast-iron skillet or cook on a hot grill for 3-4 minutes per side. When you flip the burgers, add the thinly sliced cheddar on top while the second side cooks.

3. Place the cooked burger patties on the bottom half of the toasted burger buns. Add the bacon blankets, spread the peanut butter over the bacon, add the lettuce, then tomato, and finally top with the Smoky Sriracha Mayo and relish.

Baked Parmesan Panko Pork Chops
with Quick Puttanesca Sauce

PREP TIME: **10** MINUTES | COOK TIME: **35** MINUTES | SERVES **4–6**

No need for frying. This oven-baked, lower fat pork-chop recipe is delicious served with pasta and this very quick and easy puttanesca sauce. It has been one of the most consistently popular pork-chop recipes on *RockRecipes.com* over the past 8 years and holds a very secure position in our top 25 recipes of all time.

We often serve them with whole-wheat pasta tossed with a favourite pesto for a change from the puttanesca sauce version. Either way, it's a weeknight meal your family will love.

BAKED PARMESAN PANKO PORK CHOPS

6 center-loin pork chops (¾-inch thick cut)

salt and pepper to season

⅓ cup freshly grated Parmesan cheese

1 cup panko crumbs

½ cup flour

1 egg + 1 tbsp water whisked together to make an egg wash

drizzle of olive oil

QUICK PUTTANESCA SAUCE

3 cloves garlic, minced

3 tbsp olive oil

8 large very ripe tomatoes (or one 32-oz can crushed tomatoes)

2 tbsp brown sugar

4 tbsp balsamic vinegar

½ tsp chili flakes (or to taste)

3 tbsp chopped capers (optional)

½ tsp anchovy paste (optional)

2 tbsp chopped basil

2 tbsp chopped oregano

salt and pepper to season

¼ cup chopped Kalamata olives (optional)

BAKED PARMESAN PANKO PORK CHOPS

1. Preheat oven to 375°F.

2. Season the pork chops with salt and pepper. Mix the Parmesan with the panko crumbs. Dredge the pork chops in the flour, then dip in the egg wash, and finally in the panko crumbs.

3. Place the chops on a lightly oiled baking sheet and mist or drizzle the tops with a little olive oil.

4. Bake for about 35 minutes. I like to flip the pork chops over halfway through the cooking time.

5. Use a meat thermometer to check that the center of the pork chops has reached 145°F. Let the chops rest for 5 minutes before serving with the Quick Puttanesca Sauce.

QUICK PUTTANESCA SAUCE

1. In a large sauté pan over medium heat, cook the garlic in the olive oil for only a minute. It should soften but not brown.

2. Add all of the remaining ingredients and simmer together for about 10–20 minutes, stirring often until a chunky, thick sauce develops. The amount of time this takes varies, depending on the water content of the tomatoes.

Pan-Seared Pork Chops
with Dijon Butter Sauce

PREP TIME: **10** MINUTES | COOK TIME: **20** MINUTES | SERVES **4–6**

These pan-seared pork chops show that a quick weekday meal need not be complicated or boring. These simply seasoned, pan-fried chops are complemented beautifully with a simple sauce comprised of only 4 ingredients. We often serve these juicy chops with some simple pasta that's tossed with garlic herb butter and some steamed green beans for a delicious meal in minutes.

The wine in the sauce doesn't have to be dry; a little sweetness will help balance the slight sourness of the mustard. Chicken stock can easily be substituted for the wine if you prefer.

PAN-SEARED PORK CHOPS

6–8 thick-cut pork chops

salt and pepper to season

olive oil for frying

DIJON BUTTER SAUCE

2 cloves garlic, minced

2 tbsp butter + 4 tbsp butter to finish the sauce

½ cup wine

4 tbsp whole-grain Dijon mustard

1 tbsp honey (optional)

PAN-SEARED PORK CHOPS

1. Season the pork chops with salt and pepper and pan fry in olive oil until the internal temp is 150-160°F on a meat thermometer. Hold in a warm oven (100°F) while making the sauce.

DIJON BUTTER SAUCE

1. Add the garlic and 2 tbsp butter to the sauté pan used for the chops.

2. Sauté over medium heat for only 1 minute or less to soften the garlic. (Do not let it brown.)

3. Add the wine, Dijon mustard, and honey.

4. Simmer to reduce until the sauce begins to thicken slightly.

5. Reduce heat to minimum and add the 4 tbsp butter, stirring constantly as the butter slowly melts.

6. As soon as the butter is melted, remove the sauce from the heat and serve immediately over the seared pork chops.

The Best Bolognese Sauce

PREP TIME: **30** MINUTES | COOK TIME: **3** HOURS | SERVES **8–10**

3 tbsp olive oil

6 oz finely diced pancetta or bacon

2 large onions, finely diced

6 cloves garlic, finely minced

3 celery sticks, finely diced

2 large carrots, finely diced

3 lb lean ground beef

1 tsp sea salt

1 tsp freshly ground black pepper

1 tsp freshly ground nutmeg

4 cups pureed canned tomatoes

2 cups dry red wine

3 cups low-sodium beef stock

½ cup milk

3 large bay leaves

2 lb fresh or dried pasta of your choice

1 cup freshly grated Parmesan or Romano cheese

Many people mistakenly think that Bolognese is, in essence, a tomato sauce. The Bolognese sauce that our family absolutely loves concentrates on simplicity, slow cooking, modest seasoning, and the certainty that it is most definitely a meat sauce. This recipe produces a thick, rich, simply seasoned and intensely beef-flavoured sauce. It is delicious over any pasta, in lasagna, or even used to make Bolognese Sloppy Joes!

1. In a large Dutch oven or small stock pot over medium heat, add the olive oil and chopped pancetta or bacon. Cook until the pancetta or bacon is almost crispy.

2. Add the onions, garlic, celery, and carrots and cook until the onions have softened and begin to caramelize to a light brown colour, stirring often.

3. Add the ground beef, salt, pepper, and nutmeg and cook until the beef is well browned.

4. Add the pureed tomatoes, wine, beef stock, milk, and bay leaves. Stir.

5. Cover and bring to a slow simmer.

6. Simmer very gently, stirring occasionally for 3-4 hours. If you feel you need to add more beef stock, that's fine, but you may want to turn down the heat if the liquid is boiling away too rapidly. A slow simmer is important here.

7. The liquid should be almost completely gone at the end, and the meat sauce will be quite thick. Stir in the Parmesan or Romano cheese.

8. Serve over or tossed with cooked pasta topped with lots of freshly grated Parmesan or Romano cheese.

tip > Do you throw out the rinds from Parmesan cheese? Stop! Save them in a Ziploc bag in the freezer for the next time you make Bolognese sauce and drop 2 or 3 in as soon as the sauce begins to simmer. People will wonder what the secret is to your delicious Bolognese. I waste nothing. My motto has always been, "No flavour left behind!"

Chicken Fried Pork Chops

PREP TIME: **15** MINUTES | COOK TIME: **15** MINUTES | SERVES **4–6**

If you love pork chops and are a big fan of chicken-fried steak too, this will undoubtedly become one of your favourite comfort-food meals. The pork chops stay moist and juicy when fried in the crispy herb and spice crust.

Mashed potatoes and gravy are going to be essential when serving this completely satisfying, old-fashioned, home-cooked dinner.

6 center-loin pork chops, well-trimmed

canola oil for frying

1 cup flour

2 tsp salt

2 tsp black pepper

1½ tbsp ground ginger

1 tbsp ground nutmeg

1 tsp ground thyme

1 tsp ground sage

1 tsp paprika

½ tsp cayenne pepper (or less to taste)

2 eggs + 4 tbsp water, whisked together to make an egg wash

1. Trim the pork chops well, and heat a skillet on the stove with about a half-inch of canola oil covering the bottom. You will want to carefully regulate the temperature here so the chops do not brown too quickly on the outside before they are fully cooked on the inside. I find just below medium heat works well.

2. Mix together the flour, salt, pepper, ground ginger, nutmeg, thyme, sage, paprika, and cayenne pepper until completely blended.

3. Season the pork chops with salt and pepper, then dip the chops in the flour and spice mixture. Dip the chops in the egg wash and then a final time into the flour and spice mix.

4. I use a burner setting of about 4½ out of 10 on the dial and fry them gently for about 7 or 8 minutes per side for thick pork chops. Thinner chops will take less time.

Garlic *and* Five-Spice Grilled Steak

PREP TIME: **10** MINUTES + MARINATING TIME | COOK TIME: **8** MINUTES | SERVES **4**

A super simple—and super flavourful—Asian inspired marinade makes this one of the tastiest grilled steak recipes ever. The beef can be marinated for up to 24 hours, so with a few minutes of advance preparation, this recipe will be ready to cook as soon as you can get home from work and warm up the grill. The small amount of sugar added to the marinade caramelizes and slightly chars on the surface of the meat, which is delicious with the combined flavours of soy sauce, five-spice, and garlic.

tip > As with all grilled marinated steaks, the marinating should take place in the fridge, but the steaks should be taken out of the fridge for 30-60 minutes before grilling. Grilling a cold steak can make it very difficult to cook to the perfect level and can also make your steak tougher.

4 strip loin steaks

¼ cup reduced-salt soy sauce

2 cloves garlic, minced

1 tsp Chinese five-spice powder

½ tsp black pepper

2 tbsp brown sugar

¼ tsp crushed chili flakes (optional or adjust to taste)

½ tsp toasted sesame oil (optional)

1. Trim steaks of any excess fat and place in a large Ziploc Bag.

2. Stir together all the remaining ingredients well before pouring onto the steaks and sealing the Ziploc bag. Marinate for at least an hour (and up to 24 hours) turning the Ziploc bag over a couple of times during the marinating time.

3. Preheat the grill to very high heat and grill for 4 minutes per side for medium rare steak.

4. Remove steaks from the grill and loosely cover with a sheet of aluminum foil. Rest the steaks for 5 minutes before serving.

Souvlaki Roast Pork Loin
with Lemon Oregano Tzatziki

PREP TIME: **35** MINUTES | COOK TIME: **1** HOUR **40** MINUTES | SERVES **8-10**

We absolutely love anything marinated in the flavours of Greek souvlaki at our house, and some of our versions, like chicken or steak souvlaki, have also become some of the most requested by guests at our dinner table. This particular version came about during one of those occasions when I was looking for a shortcut way of feeding souvlaki to a large crowd. The sliced pork roast is terrific to serve with tzatziki, Greek salad, and the Lemon Herb Roasted Potato Nuggets on (page 140) for a complete dinner. Thin slices with Greek salad and tzatziki on fresh flatbread or pita bread make fantastically delicious wraps too, even with the leftovers.

SOUVLAKI ROAST PORK LOIN

2 tbsp fresh lemon juice

3 tbsp balsamic vinegar

1 tsp kosher salt

3 rounded tbsp smoked paprika

2 tsp freshly ground black pepper

6 cloves garlic, minced

a little olive oil

3–4 lb center-loin roast of pork

LEMON OREGANO TZATZIKI

3 cups Greek yogurt, drained.

6 inch piece of English cucumber

1 tsp kosher salt

3 tbsp finely chopped fresh oregano

2 cloves garlic, minced

3 tbsp fresh lemon juice

1 tsp finely minced lemon zest

2 tbsp olive oil

pinch salt and pepper

SOUVLAKI ROAST PORK LOIN

1. Preheat oven to 350°F.

2. Mix together the lemon juice, balsamic vinegar, salt, smoked paprika, pepper and garlic.

3. Add only enough olive oil to bring the mixture to a brushable paste.

4. Rub or brush the paste all over the surface of the pork-loin roast. Let it sit in the fridge for 30 minutes.

5. Roast in the preheated oven for about 25 minutes per pound, until a meat thermometer reaches 160°F for well-cooked but still juicy pork.

6. Tent the cooked pork roast loosely with aluminum foil and let rest for 10-15 minutes before thinly slicing and serving with the Lemon Oregano Tzatziki.

LEMON OREGANO TZATZIKI

1. Draining the yogurt removes much of the liquid and produces an end product about the consistency of thick sour cream. To drain the yogurt, line a colander with several layers of cheese-cloth (or in a pinch, several large coffee filters). Pour the yogurt into the colander and place it in a large bowl or in the sink for an hour or two. This should produce about 2 cups of thick yogurt.

2.   Peel the piece of cucumber and remove the seeds and pulp at the center with a teaspoon, then dice the outside flesh of the cucumber into small cubes of ⅛ inch or less.

3.   Sprinkle the kosher salt over the diced cucumber and toss together well. Let this rest for about 30 minutes, stirring occasionally. This process removes some of the liquid from the cucumber so that it will not water down the consistency of your finished tzatziki.

4.   Drain all of the liquid off the diced cucumber before adding it to the drained yogurt along with the oregano, minced garlic, lemon juice, lemon zest, olive oil, salt, and pepper.

5.   Mix well, cover, and store in the fridge for at least 30 minutes before serving.

Parmesan Panko Crusted Rack of Lamb

PREP TIME: **20** MINUTES | COOK TIME: **35** MINUTES | SERVES **2**

RACK OF LAMB

1 large rack of lamb, at least 8 ribs

¼ tsp black pepper

¼ tsp salt

1 tbsp Dijon mustard

⅓ cup panko crumbs

¼ cup grated Parmesan cheese

1 tbsp chopped fresh rosemary

COUNTRY CROUTONS

3 cups diced-large crusty bread

½ cup milk

3 tbsp olive oil

3 tbsp butter

1 clove garlic, minced

1½ tbsp chopped fresh rosemary

¼ tsp salt

¼ tsp black pepper

¼ cup beef, veal, or chicken stock

ROSEMARY DIJON DRESSING

1 clove garlic, finely minced

1 tbsp capers

1 tbsp chopped fresh rosemary

4 tbsp olive oil

1½ tbsp Dijon mustard

2 anchovy fillets or
1 tbsp anchovy paste

2 tbsp apple cider vinegar

1 tbsp honey

Lamb was always a bit of a treat for me at our house because Spouse and the kids were never very fond of it. This is the recipe that changed their minds.

This rack of lamb gets cooked to a perfect medium rare with a crispy exterior crust. The bed of country croutons and the rosemary Dijon dressing served with the lamb provide a complementary, stuffing-like side dish. All that's really needed are some simple steamed vegetables to complete a meal worthy of any celebration dinner.

RACK OF LAMB

1. Preheat oven to 425°F.

2. Season the lamb with salt and pepper and brush on the Dijon mustard.

3. Toss together the panko, Parmesan, and rosemary, and roll the lamb rack in the mixture, pressing it onto the meat to get good contact.

4. Roast, bone-side down, for 10 minutes and then reduce the heat to 350°F and roast for about 15-25 minutes longer until the internal temperature reaches 130°F for rare, 140°F for medium rare, or 160°F for well done.

5. Let the meat rest for 10 minutes after it comes out of the oven before carving and serving with the Country Croutons and Rosemary Dijon Dressing.

COUNTRY CROUTONS

1. Bread that is a couple of days old is best for this purpose. Pour the milk over the bread, toss and drain off the excess milk, if any.

2. Add the olive oil and butter to a large sauté pan over medium heat. The pan should be big enough to accommodate

the bread cubes in a single layer. Add the garlic, and sauté for only a minute before adding the soaked bread cubes. Add the rosemary, salt, and pepper and toss well before spreading the cubes out in a single layer.

3. Pour the stock into the pan and let it boil off, leaving the cubes to brown on one side before turning them several times as they brown and get crispy.

ROSEMARY DIJON DRESSING

1. Combine all ingredients together in a blender at low speed for about 30 seconds. Drizzle over the croutons and rack of lamb.

Regular readers of *RockRecipes.com* know how much I love seafood, so this chapter was a great excuse to indulge that passion. I got to cook and reshoot some of the most popular seafood recipes from the past, plus develop some brand new ones just for this book. Whether it's using traditional Newfoundland fish cakes as the base for a great brunch dish or mastering a creamy, flavourful scallop and bacon risotto, you'll find plenty of inspiration to indulge your seafood passion too.

seafood

Newfoundland Fish Cakes 62

Manhattan Style Roasted Vegetable Chorizo Seafood Chowder 64

Mussels Marinara 66

Chicken Fried Cod Nuggets *with* Lime Chive Mayo 68

Roasted Tomato Fennel Lobster Bisque. 70

Popcorn Shrimp *with* Chili Lime Dipping Sauce 72

Salmon in Pastry *with* Dijon Cream Sauce 74

Seafood Shells and Cheese. 76

Quidi Vidi Beer Battered Shrimp *with* Chili Lime or Lime Curry Mayo 78

Tarragon and Chive Pan-Fried Cod *with* Fettuccine Puttanesca 80

Bacon Fennel Risotto *with* Seared Scallops. 82

Newfoundland Fish Cakes

PREP TIME: 30 MINUTES + SOAKING TIME | **COOK TIME: 15 MINUTES** | **MAKES 8 LARGE CAKES**

Still popular today, this very simple dish was a staple on many Newfoundland kitchen tables for probably hundreds of years, given that the simple ingredients were readily available from the land and the sea. I remember my grandmothers cooking them in large cast-iron skillets in the rendered fat from making scrunchions. For non-native readers, scrunchions are a very traditional accompaniment to several traditional Newfoundland meals and are simply small cubes of cured fat-back pork fried until crispy to render out most of the fat.

These fish cakes make a terrific lunch with a simple salad or served with poached eggs as a tasty weekend brunch idea.

1½ lb salt dried cod

¼ cup butter

1 small onion, chopped

6 cups mashed potato

1 beaten egg

½ tsp black pepper

2 tbsp dried savoury (optional)

about ½ cup all-purpose flour

canola oil for frying

1. Soak the salt cod in cold water overnight.

2. After soaking, simmer the salt cod in boiling water for about 15 minutes. Drain the water off the fish and allow the fish to cool to almost room temperature.

3. When the fish is cool, flake it apart with a fork into small pieces.

4. In a sauté pan, melt the butter over medium heat.

5. Add the onion and cook until softened.

6. Add the flaked fish along with the mashed potato, egg, pepper, and savoury.

7. Mix together until well combined, then form into small cakes and roll in flour.

8. Fry the fish cakes in canola oil over medium heat until golden brown on both sides.

9. Serve with scrunchions if desired.

> tip > I've also made these with leftover fresh cod, which I actually prefer when using them for brunch with poached eggs and Hollandaise sauce.

Manhattan Style Roasted Vegetable Chorizo Seafood Chowder

PREP TIME: **30** MINUTES | COOK TIME: **30** MINUTES | SERVES **6–8**

½ fennel bulb, chopped

1 medium red onion, chopped

2 carrots, chopped

2 parsnips, chopped

1 red bell pepper, chopped

2 stalks celery, chopped

3 tbsp olive oil

salt and pepper to season

6 slices of smoked bacon, chopped in small pieces

4 oz of chopped, Spanish style, hard chorizo sausage

2 tbsp olive oil

3 cloves garlic, minced

1 large shallot, finely chopped

¾ cup dry white wine

3 cups tomato juice

3 cups fish stock (or chicken stock if you prefer)

3 cups vegetable stock

1 bay leaf

2 tsp chopped fresh thyme

2 tsp marjoram or oregano

2 tsp smoked paprika

salt and pepper to season

3 Roma tomatoes, chopped

2 lb of seafood of your choice: clams, mussels, scallops, and shrimp are great choices. Cut fish such as cod, salmon, or halibut into bite-sized pieces

I love a creamy chowder as much as anyone, but sometimes the richness of a cream or roux thickened chowder can be quite heavy, especially when you're featuring the delicate flavours of several different types of seafood in the same dish. This Manhattan style chowder is my replication of one I tasted in the Boston area many years ago. It was served as an appetizer course and featured only scallops and shrimp, but the chef had added some chopped spicy chorizo sausage to the broth. Everyone knows I have a thing for smoky flavours, so it's no surprise I fell in love with the idea.

Make this outstanding chowder as simple as you like by choosing one or two of your favourite seafood choices, or go all out for a total celebration meal that includes as many seafood varieties as you can fit in the pot. I like to serve it with some freshly baked pieces of crusty French baguette for soaking up the smoky, deeply flavourful broth. All the seafood is simply poached in the rich broth at the end, and the same can be done for scallops if you are using them, but I like to pan sear those separately and add them when serving for a particularly appealing presentation.

1.   Preheat oven to 375°F.

2.   Start by roasting the vegetables. Chop the fennel, onions, carrots, parsnips, red bell pepper, and celery into bite-sized pieces. Toss the vegetables in 3 tbsp olive oil, season in salt and pepper, and bake in a single layer on a cookie sheet for 20-30 minutes or until the vegetables are slightly browned and fork tender. Turn the vegetables once during the cooking time.

3. In a sauté pan, cook the bacon to crisp. In the last few minutes of cooking the bacon, add the chopped chorizo sausage. Drain off the fat.

4. In a large pot or large Dutch oven over medium heat, add the olive oil, garlic, and shallots and sauté for just a minute to soften them. Add the white wine and simmer gently until reduced to about half the volume.

5. Add the roasted vegetables along with the previously cooked bacon and sausage to the tomato juice, fish stock, vegetable stock, bay leaf, thyme, marjoram, smoked paprika, a pinch of salt and pepper, and the Roma tomatoes. Simmer very gently for 20-30 minutes.

6. Add the seafood and bring the chowder back up to a very slow simmer. Cover and let the fish and shellfish simmer for 10 minutes. Serve immediately.

Mussels Marinara

PREP TIME: **10** MINUTES | COOK TIME: **20** MINUTES | SERVES **4**

Mussels, I think, are an underutilized seafood when it comes to everyday dinners and special occasions. I love them because, like clams and oysters, they're sold while still alive and really do deliver some of the freshest seafood flavour to be found. When you open a bag of fresh mussels, it just smells like fresh sea air.

In aquaculture, mussels are very easy to grow and therefore quite an economical option too. Despite being inexpensive in comparison to other seafood, I think they still look quite impressive when served in a dish like this super-easy Mussels Marinara. Beautiful looking and delicious meals like this one, which are so quick and easy to prepare, are always my favourite to serve when having guests. Maximum visual and flavour impact with minimum effort is always a recipe for successful entertaining.

2 to 3 lb fresh mussels

¾ lb dry linguine

6 cloves garlic, minced

2 tbsp olive oil

6 large tomatoes, finely diced (or 2 cups canned crushed tomatoes)

2 cups seafood stock (or vegetable stock)

¼ cup dry red wine

1 tbsp brown sugar

½ tsp chili flakes (more or less to taste)

½ tsp chili flakes (optional)

½ tsp black pepper

pinch salt

¼ cup grated Parmesan cheese

3 tbsp chopped fresh basil

1. Before cooking this dish, prepare the mussels to be added at the end. Wash the mussels and pull off any beards that may still be attached to the shell. A pair of needle-nose pliers works well for this. Discard any mussels with cracked or broken shells and those that do not remain closed after a minute when you pinch them together. Also discard any mussels that do not open during the cooking time.

2. Cook the linguine in salted water to al dente, about 8-10 minutes or as directed. It's important not to overcook the linguine.

3. In a large covered pot or Dutch oven over medium heat, add the garlic and olive oil and sauté for just a minute to soften the garlic.

4. Add the tomatoes, seafood stock, red wine, brown sugar, chili flakes, pepper, and salt. Increase the heat and simmer rapidly for about 5 minutes to reduce the sauce.

5. Reduce the heat to medium-low and add the mussels. Cover and let the mussels steam for 8-10 minutes, depending on their size.

6. Remove the mussels to a platter and add the cooked linguine and Parmesan cheese. Toss together so the sauce coats the pasta well.

7. Serve the pasta with the mussels and a garnish of the fresh chopped basil and a little extra Parmesan cheese.

Chicken Fried Cod Nuggets
with Lime Chive Mayo

PREP TIME: **20** MINUTES | COOK TIME: **6** MINUTES | SERVES **4**

CHICKEN FRIED COD NUGGETS

2 lb cod fillets

kosher salt to season

egg wash (2 eggs + 4 tbsp milk)

2 cups flour

2 tsp freshly grated nutmeg

1 tsp cayenne pepper (or less to taste)

2 tsp salt

2 tsp freshly ground black pepper

1 tbsp dry ground thyme

1 tbsp dry ground oregano

vegetable oil for deep frying

LIME CHIVE MAYO

2 large or extra-large egg yolks

¾ tsp salt

1 tsp sugar

pinch cayenne pepper

zest of 1 lime, finely chopped

1 cup light olive oil

juice of 1 large lime

2 tbsp chopped chives

This recipe was inspired by leftovers! There were a couple of leftover fish fillets from a stuffed cod recipe, some leftover flour and spice dredge from a chicken-fried steak, and some leftover homemade lime and chive mayo from the crab cakes I'd cooked the day before. Nothing ever goes to waste in my house, so I used them all to create this new fried-fish recipe. It turned out crispy and delicious. The fish stayed very moist inside, and the tangy lime mayo made a nice alternative to tartar sauce. The whole family enjoyed it so much that we've been making it ever since. That's the kind of reward that can happen when you put a little creativity into the ingredients you already have on hand and commit to minimal food waste.

CHICKEN FRIED COD NUGGETS

1. Cut the cod fillets into 2-inch square-ish pieces. Lightly season the fish pieces with kosher salt.

2. Whisk the eggs and milk together to make an egg wash.

3. To make a flour dredge, mix together the flour, nutmeg, cayenne pepper, salt, pepper, thyme and oregano.

4. Dip the cod pieces into the flour dredge and press the mixture firmly on all sides of the fish. Shake off the excess flour and dip the pieces into the egg wash.

5. Return the egg washed pieces of fish back to the flour dredge and toss well to coat them on all sides.

6. Preheat deep fryer to 350°F and drop the cod nuggets in.

7. Fry for about 4-6 minutes until a medium golden brown.

8. Drain on a wire rack placed on a cookie sheet. Hold in a 175°F oven if making more than one batch. Serve with Lime Chive Mayo.

LIME CHIVE MAYO

1. In a blender on medium-high speed, combine the egg yolks, salt, sugar, cayenne pepper, and lime zest until thick and pale in colour.

2. Add the olive oil alternately with lime juice in three parts, adding the oil very slowly in a thin stream. This will produce a thick mayonnaise. Fold in the chopped chives and serve.

Roasted Tomato Fennel Lobster Bisque

PREP TIME: **1** HOUR | COOK TIME: **1** HOUR **30** MINUTES | SERVES **6-8**

LOBSTER

3 lb lobster in the shell

SEAFOOD STOCK

shells from the cooked lobster

2 cups of the liquid the lobster is boiled in

6 cups water

1 small onion, chopped

3 cloves garlic, roughly chopped

3 tbsp chopped tarragon or dill

2 stalks celery, roughly chopped

1 carrot, roughly chopped

6 peppercorns

ROASTED TOMATOES AND FENNEL

8 large ripe tomatoes, diced

1 large fennel bulb, diced

1 medium red onion, diced

2 cloves garlic, chopped

4 tbsp olive oil

2 tbsp honey

3 tbsp balsamic vinegar

salt and pepper to season

6 cups of Seafood Stock

2 tbsp chopped fresh tarragon (dill is good too)

1 squeeze of fresh lemon

drizzle of heavy cream

This beautiful soup was created in homage to the first lobster bisque I ever tasted, which was served at Chateau Montebello Hotel in Quebec many years ago. I was very impressed by the rich soup with the lightly herbed flavour of tarragon. I credit that bisque with opening my eyes to seafood such as lobster and crab, which I avoided as a child. We would have massive crab boils in particular at our house when I was growing up, but my parents could never get me to partake. I guess I'm well over that stage now, hey Mom and Dad?

Small cups of this soup make a wonderful first course at any dinner party or celebratory meal. It would also be the star of the show if served as the main course at a special lunch.

LOBSTER

1. Begin cooking the lobster by dropping it into salted boiling water. Don't overcook the lobster; a little underdone is probably best because it will be added back to the hot bisque. For 1½ lb lobsters, about 8 minutes is good. Save 2 cups of the water in which the lobster is cooked.

SEAFOOD STOCK

1. Shell the lobster over a large bowl to catch any liquid. Separate the meat from the body and claws and chop it into a ½-inch dice to add back to the bisque later. Whole, shelled claws on top of the soup make a beautiful, impressive presentation.

2. Simmer the shells and any liquid in the bowl along with the 2 cups of the steaming liquid and the 6 cups water, onion, garlic, tarragon, celery, carrot, and peppercorns.

3. Simmer very gently together for about 30-45 minutes. Strain through several layers of cheesecloth to create a clear broth. While the stock simmers, get started on the roasted tomatoes and fennel.

ROASTED TOMATOES AND FENNEL

1. Preheat oven to 350°F.

2. Toss together the diced tomatoes, fennel, onion, garlic, olive oil, honey, balsamic vinegar, salt and pepper.

3. Bake in a shallow baking dish for about 60-70 minutes, stirring occasionally or until the fennel pieces are very soft, most of the liquid has cooked off, and the tomato and fennel reach a good chunky consistency. Puree this mixture well in a blender or food processor and pour into a soup pot.

4. Add 6 cups of the seafood stock and 2 tbsp chopped tarragon to the soup. Simmer on medium-low heat for 20-30 minutes or until the soup reaches your desired consistency.

5. Taste and do a final seasoning of salt and pepper if necessary.

6. Add the chopped lobster meat to the soup and simmer for just a couple of minutes before doing a final seasoning of salt and pepper, stirring in a squeeze of lemon and serving with a drizzle of heavy cream. Whole, shelled claws on top of the soup make a beautiful, impressive presentation if you want to fully cook some separately for this purpose.

Popcorn Shrimp *with* Chili Lime Dipping Sauce

PREP TIME: **20** MINUTES | COOK TIME: **20** MINUTES | SERVES **4**

CHILI LIME DIPPING SAUCE

1 clove garlic, minced

1 tbsp olive oil

½ cup honey

⅔ cup water

1 tsp crushed chili paste (or ½ tsp chili flakes) or adjust to taste

juice of 2 limes

zest of 1 lime, finely minced

pinch of salt

¼ tsp black pepper

2 tsp cornstarch

1 oz water

POPCORN SHRIMP

1 cup flour

½ tsp salt

¼ tsp pepper

1½ tbsp powdered ginger

1 lb large uncooked shrimp (about 21–25 shrimp)

egg wash (2 eggs + 4 tbsp water)

vegetable oil for frying

This is the kind of recipe that does double duty at our house. It's one of my most requested party foods, and it's great to serve when friends just come over for drinks. It's also great game-day food, and I've heard from many readers who add these crunchy shrimp morsels to their annual Super Bowl celebrations.

With shrimp this tasty, though, you can't wait around for a special occasion to serve them. Sometimes I double the sauce recipe and serve the shrimp with plain steamed rice as a scrumptious dinner idea. The extra sauce gets served over the rice, and we most often add steamed snow peas as a side to complete the delicious meal.

CHILI LIME DIPPING SAUCE

1. In a small saucepan over medium heat, sauté the garlic in the olive oil just for a minute to soften it, but don't let it brown.

2. Add the honey, water, crushed chili paste, lime juice, lime zest, salt, and pepper and bring to a slow simmer for 5 minutes.

3. Dissolve the cornstarch in the 1 oz of water and pour into the boiling mixture while stirring constantly. Boil for 30 seconds or so before removing from the heat and serving.

POPCORN SHRIMP

1. Mix together the flour, salt, pepper, and ginger.

2. Cut the shrimp into about 2 or 3 pieces each and season lightly with salt.

3. Make an egg wash by whisking together the 2 eggs and 4 tbsp water.

4. Dip the shrimp into the flour mixture to coat well, pressing the flour mixture firmly onto all sides of the shrimp pieces. Quickly dip the floured pieces into the egg wash and then back for a final toss in the flour dredge.

5. Preheat fryer to 375°F. Remove the coated shrimp pieces from the flour dredge and drop them into the preheated fryer.

6. Fry just until light golden brown, only about 4-5 minutes maximum. Serve with the dipping sauce.

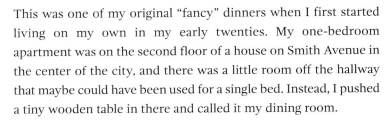

Salmon in Pastry *with* Dijon Cream Sauce

SALMON IN PASTRY

1 cup very cold butter

1½ cups all-purpose flour

½ tsp salt

½ cup sour cream

1½ lb boneless, skinless salmon fillet

salt and pepper to season

1 lemon wedge

2 tbsp chopped fresh dill or tarragon

egg wash (1 egg + 1 tbsp water)

DIJON CREAM SAUCE

2 tbsp olive oil

3 cloves garlic, minced

⅓ cup white wine

1½ cups whipping cream

3 tbsp Dijon mustard

3 tbsp fresh chopped tarragon

salt and pepper to season

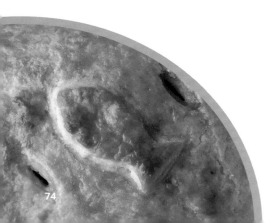

This was one of my original "fancy" dinners when I first started living on my own in my early twenties. My one-bedroom apartment was on the second floor of a house on Smith Avenue in the center of the city, and there was a little room off the hallway that maybe could have been used for a single bed. Instead, I pushed a tiny wooden table in there and called it my dining room.

The kitchen wasn't much bigger, but that didn't stop me from inviting over 6 or more people and cramming them into that tiny room for dinner parties. Those early guests probably all sampled this indulgent salmon recipe back then, and I still get asked to make it today. I love that it's one of those main courses you can prep in advance, keep in the fridge, and then pop into a hot oven once your guests arrive. After all, dinner parties should be about spending time with people, not in the kitchen.

SALMON IN PASTRY

1.   Cut butter into the flour and salt with a food processor or pastry blender until mixture resembles a coarse meal. Small pieces of butter should still be visible in the mix.

2.   Stir in the sour cream to form a dough. Form dough into a rough rectangle about 1 inch thick, wrap it in plastic, and rest in the fridge for 20 minutes.

3.   Roll the dough out into a rectangle about 2-3 inches longer than the salmon fillet you are using and a bit more than twice the width of the piece of fish. (Alternatively you can roll the dough into 4 smaller rectangles and prepare the servings individually.) If necessary, fold the thinnest tail section of the fish under the fillet to make it approximately the same thickness throughout.

4.   Place salmon on one half the pastry.

5. Season the salmon with salt and pepper and a squeeze of lemon from the wedge. Sprinkle the salmon with dill or tarragon.

6. Fold the dough over the salmon and pinch the edges together to seal. Brush the top of the pastry with an egg wash made from 1 beaten egg and 1 tbsp water. Cut a couple of small slits in the top of the pastry with the tip of a sharp knife.

7. Chill for at least 30 minutes.

8. Preheat oven to 375°F then bake for 30-40 minutes, depending on the thickness of the salmon, until the pastry is a uniform golden brown.

DIJON CREAM SAUCE

1. In a small saucepan over medium heat, sauté the olive oil and garlic for only a minute to soften but not brown the garlic. Add the wine.

2. Simmer until volume of wine is reduced by half, then add the whipping cream, Dijon mustard, chopped tarragon, and a pinch of salt and pepper.

3. Simmer very slowly until sauce thickens enough to coat a metal spoon. Serve with the salmon.

Seafood Shells and Cheese

PREP TIME: **40** MINUTES | COOK TIME: **45** MINUTES | SERVES **4** (**8 AS AN APPETIZER**)

SEAFOOD SHELLS AND CHEESE

2 cups medium-sized shell pasta (uncooked)

1 lb seafood (either shrimp, lobster, crab, scallops)

2½ cups whole milk

3 tbsp butter

2 tbsp flour

¼ tsp black pepper

½ tsp sea salt

4 oz smoked Gruyere cheese, grated (You can substitute Asiago, Parmesan, or Romano)

1 tsp fresh chopped tarragon or dill

2 tbsp Dijon mustard (preferably whole grain)

4 oz grated mozzarella

4 oz grated Monterey Jack, Emmental, Swiss or Jarlsberg Cheese, your preference.

CRUMB TOPPING

1 cup cracker or bread crumbs (I use Ritz cracker crumbs)

½ cup ground almonds

2 tbsp melted butter

1 tsp chopped tarragon

pinch of cracked black pepper

This recipe is basically an elevated version of mac & cheese, taking the classic comfort food to a whole new level. It's a versatile dish that can be combined with any seafood you like really. I most often make it very simply with shrimp for an inexpensive indulgence, but you could easily use lobster, scallops, or crab as well. For special occasions, a combination of any of those would be incredibly delicious.

I love the flavour note of the smoked cheese in this recipe, but if that isn't to your taste, just use an un-smoked variety. Milder cheeses will work best, so substitute another and make the dish your own.

1. Preheat oven to 375°F.

2. Cook the pasta in salted boiling water to al dente. Do not overcook. Slightly undercooked would be preferable.

3. Begin by lightly steaming the seafood. It's important not to overcook the seafood for this recipe. Under cooking it by 5 minutes or so is preferable because the seafood does get reheated and cooks somewhat in the oven as well. Shrimp and scallops can be used uncooked if you prefer. Uncooked large shrimp or medium-size scallops or large chunks of cooked lobster, crab, or cod or a combination of all work well.

4. While you prepare the sauce, scald the milk in the microwave or on the stovetop to almost boiling.

5. In a medium saucepan over medium heat, cook together the butter, flour, pepper, and sea salt for 2 minutes.

6. Whisking constantly, slowly pour in scalded milk. Continue to cook for 2 more minutes, stirring constantly.

7. Remove from heat and stir in the Gruyere cheese, tarragon, and Dijon mustard. Set aside.

8. Grate the other cheeses, mix them together and set aside.

9. Grease an 8-10 cup casserole dish well with butter (or 4 large individual gratin dishes).

10. Place ⅓ of the pasta in the bottom of the dish.

11. Pour on ⅓ the sauce.

12. Scatter half the seafood over the surface.

13. Repeat the layers ending with the grated cheese on the top.

14. Mix all of the ingredients for the crumb topping together and sprinkle evenly over the grated cheese.

15. Cover casserole dish and bake for 30 minutes. Uncover and cook for 15 minutes longer.

Quidi Vidi Beer Battered Shrimp
with Chili Lime or Lime Curry Mayo

PREP TIME: **20** MINUTES | COOK TIME: **10** MINUTES | SERVES **4**

BEER BATTERED SHRIMP

1 tsp instant dry yeast (the type that can be directly added to flour and does not need proofing in water first)

½ tsp sea salt

1¼ cups flour, sifted

3 tbsp warm water

one 12 oz bottle Quidi Vidi 1892 Traditional Ale at room temperature

vegetable oil for deep frying

2 dozen fresh, raw, large shrimp (peeled, washed, and de-veined)

1 tsp sea salt

¼ tsp pepper

½ cup flour

CHILI LIME OR LIME CURRY MAYO

2 large or extra-large egg yolks

¾ tsp salt

1 tsp sugar

a pinch cayenne pepper

½ tsp finely minced lime zest

about 1 cup light olive oil

juice of 1 large lime

1 tsp curry powder or 1 tsp chili sauce (more or less to taste)

This beer batter is different than some I've tried in that it uses yeast. I was quite pleased with the result the first time I tried it because not only did it taste wonderful, but the batter remained crispy after deep frying and did not get soggy at all. The flavour of Quidi Vidi Breweries 1892 Traditional Ale in the batter no doubt had plenty to do with its great taste. A beer with flavour is important to the recipe, so choose a premium light or amber coloured ale or lager if you can. I'm sure there's a local favourite.

As always, deep frying in small batches and keeping the heat well regulated to maintain 375°F is crucial to a crispy final product that has not absorbed a lot of oil in the cooking process. This is a recipe I use mostly as finger food at parties, but sometimes we throw a few home fries next to them and they make a tasty lunch or dinner too. At parties, I like to serve both versions of the mayo because I think most people will like one or the other or both.

BEER BATTERED SHRIMP

1. Add the instant yeast and sea salt to the flour and stir together. Add the water and beer and whisk together well. The Beer Batter should be thin like pancake batter. If the Beer Batter appears too thick or too thin, you can add a little more flour or water as needed. Don't worry if there are still a few lumps in the batter: this is not a problem. It's better not to over mix this batter.

2. Set the batter aside to rest for 10 minutes.

3. Heat the vegetable oil in a deep fryer to 375°F.

4. Toss the shrimp in the salt and pepper and then dredge them well in the flour before dipping them into the Beer Batter and dropping them into the hot oil.

5. Cook until golden brown, turning them over once if necessary.

6. Remove from oil and rest on a wire rack for 5 minutes to cool slightly before serving with the mayo.

CHILI LIME OR LIME CURRY MAYO

1. In a blender on medium-high speed, combine the egg yolks, salt, sugar, cayenne pepper, and lime zest until thick and pale in colour.

2. Add the olive oil alternately with the lime juice in three parts, adding the oil very slowly in a thin stream. Add only enough oil to make a thin mayonnaise about the consistency of Hollandaise sauce. Stir in the curry powder or chili sauce and serve with the Beer Battered Shrimp.

Tarragon and Chive Pan-Fried Cod
with Fettuccine Puttanesca

PREP TIME: **15** MINUTES | COOK TIME: **15** MINUTES | SERVES **4**

TARRAGON AND CHIVE PAN-FRIED COD

1½ lb **cod**, cut into small evenly sized pieces

salt and **pepper** to season

1 tbsp chopped **chives**

1 tbsp chopped **tarragon**

1 cup **flour**

1 tsp **salt**

½ tsp **black pepper**

vegetable oil for frying

PUTTANESCA SAUCE

4 tbsp **olive oil**

4 **cloves garlic**, chopped

6 **large fresh tomatoes**, chopped (or a dozen Roma tomatoes)

1 tsp **anchovy paste** or 2 **anchovy fillets**, chopped (optional)

3 tbsp chopped **fresh tarragon** (or 1½ tbsp dried tarragon)

3 tbsp chopped **chives**

1 tsp **brown sugar**

2 tbsp roughly chopped **capers** (optional)

salt and **pepper** to season

pinch **dried chili flakes** (or crushed chili paste to taste)

½ cup **pitted Kalamata olives**

one 12-oz package of **fresh fettuccine pasta**

Pan-fried cod is a staple meal in so many homes in Newfoundland, and for good reason. The simple traditional preparation of freshly caught cod fillets, dredged in flour and quickly fried in rendered fat-back pork, is simple deliciousness at its best.

Pasta Puttanesca is a staple at our house and has been for years. The very quickly cooked pasta sauce made from fresh tomatoes is extremely versatile, and we often add quickly sautéed shrimp or scallops for a quick meal, so I thought, "Why not little bites of pan-fried cod?" I chose some non-traditional herbs to pair with the fish, and it turned out that the bright, fresh flavour of the easy to prepare tomato sauce was delicious without overwhelming the delicate cod flavour. I'm a huge fan of seafood and pasta dishes, and this one is highly recommended. It may just become one of your family's favourites too.

TARRAGON AND CHIVE PAN-FRIED COD

1. Heat a large sauté pan or cast-iron pan on a setting between medium and medium-high heat.

2. Lightly season the cod pieces with salt and pepper and toss them with the fresh chives and tarragon.

3. Mix together the flour, salt, and black pepper to form a dredge for the fish.

4. Dredge the cod pieces in the flour mixture. Cover the bottom of the heated pan with vegetable oil and let it heat up for a minute before frying the cod pieces to golden brown: only a few minutes per side, turning only once.

PUTTANESCA SAUCE

1. Add the olive oil and garlic to a separate large sauté pan over medium to medium-high heat. Sauté for only a minute to soften the garlic, but don't let it brown.

2. Add the tomatoes, anchovy paste, tarragon, chives, brown sugar, capers, salt, pepper, and chili flakes.

3. Simmer together, stirring occasionally for only about 10 minutes or until the tomatoes break down a little and a sauce forms. The tomatoes will still be quite chunky, but most of the liquid should simmer off. In the last 1-2 minutes of cooking, add the olives.

4. Cook the fettuccine to al dente in salted water as directed on the package. I like to use fresh pasta for this recipe which only takes 5 minutes or less to boil. Serve cod pieces and sauce over the cooked fettuccine and top with freshly grated Parmesan cheese.

Bacon Fennel Risotto *with* Seared Scallops

PREP TIME: **15** MINUTES | COOK TIME: **35** MINUTES | SERVES **4**

A quick thumb through this cookbook and it won't be hard to guess that scallops are my favourite seafood. The hardest part about writing the seafood recipes for this book was trying to pick my very favourite scallop recipes. I may have gone a little overboard, but I couldn't resist adding just one more. I particularly wanted to add this one to dispel the myth that risotto is difficult to make. It's not. There is no particular skill required, just time and, just as importantly, attention. It's a dish that requires constant stirring and judgment, but you will master it quickly and reap the creamy, delicious, savoury reward in the end.

3½–4 cups low-sodium seafood or chicken stock

½ cup white wine

4 slices smoked bacon, crisp-cooked and chopped

4 tbsp extra-virgin olive oil

½ cup finely diced Spanish onion

½ cup finely diced fennel

3 cloves garlic, minced

salt and pepper to season

½ cup Arborio rice, no substitutes

¼ cup finely grated Parmesan cheese

2 tbsp butter to finish the risotto

1 dozen large scallops

2 tbsp butter + 2 tbsp olive oil for searing the scallops

1. Add the seafood stock and white wine to a small saucepan and bring to a very slow simmer. Maintain the stock at a boiling temperature.

2. While the stock heats, crisp cook the bacon in a medium-sized saucepan. Remove and set aside. Reserve a couple of tablespoons of bacon for garnish.

3. Pour off most of the bacon fat and add the 4 tbsp olive oil to the pan over medium-low heat. Add the onions, fennel, and garlic. Slowly sauté until the onions soften but do not brown. Season lightly with a little salt and pepper.

4. Add the rice. Sauté together for 3-5 minutes to completely coat the rice.

5. Add one cup of the stock/wine mixture and stir in. Adjust the heat so the risotto very slowly simmers.

6. Continue to stir the risotto constantly as it begins to thicken. After about 5 minutes, when the risotto begins to thicken, add another cup of the stock/wine mixture. Repeat this process about 4 times. Add the bacon when about half of the stock has been used.

7. Taste the risotto to see if the rice is fully cooked and to see if the risotto needs any more seasoning. Add a little more stock and continue to stir if the rice is still a little hard.

8. Add the grated Parmesan cheese and stir in until smooth. Add the butter here to finish off the risotto.

9. Serve immediately, topped with pan-seared scallops and a garnish of crisp bacon and chives or fennel fronds.

10. To pan sear the scallops, make sure they are at close to room temperature, so take them out of the fridge about 20 minutes in advance.

11. Heat the oil and butter for searing over medium-high heat in a non-stick skillet. Pan sear the scallops for only 2-3 minutes per side, depending on their size.

If there's one thing I've proven for certain in the past eight years of writing a recipe blog, it's that weekday meals do not need to be boring. I've published hundreds of such recipes, and I think the most gratifying comments come from people who take the time to tell me how much their family loved one of my quick and easy dinners. From quick pasta dishes and stir fries to healthy salads, flavour never takes a backseat to how quickly these dishes can be prepared.

quick and easy dinners

Easy Five-Spice Ginger Beef 86

Creamy Lemon Pepper Scallops Linguine 88

Thirty Minute Easy Chicken *and* Chickpea Curry 90

Mediterranean Lemon Butter Chicken 92

Low-Fat Ranch Chicken Salad 94

Smoked Chicken, Spinach, Grilled Pineapple, and Pomegranate Salad 96

Low-Fat Chicken Taco Salad *with* Mango Salsa 98

Cherry Orange Pork Medallions 100

Mediterranean Lemon Chicken Orzo Salad 102

Low-Fat Turkey Sausage *and* Brown Rice 104

White Bean Chicken Chili 106

Orange Mint Grilled Shrimp 108

Parmesan Bacon Chicken Linguine 110

Easy Five-Spice Ginger Beef

PREP TIME: **10** MINUTES | COOK TIME: **10** MINUTES | SERVES **4**

2 thick-cut strip-loin steaks, well-trimmed and thinly sliced

salt and pepper to season

3 tbsp + 2 tbsp peanut oil

4 cloves garlic, minced

½ cup orange juice

½ cup hoisin sauce

3 tbsp grated fresh ginger

1 tsp Chinese five-spice powder

4 tbsp molasses (or substitute honey)

1 tsp crushed chili paste

4 tbsp rice wine vinegar

2 tbsp soy sauce

½ tsp cracked black pepper

3 tsp toasted sesame oil

cornstarch slurry (1 rounded tbsp cornstarch dissolved in 1 oz cold water)

1 red bell pepper, chopped

This is the kind of meal you could expect to find at our place if you showed up unexpectedly for dinner, and I'm pretty sure you wouldn't be disappointed. It might be ready in a flash, but it's also full of great Asian flavours.

As with all stir-fried Asian dishes, it's always best to assemble your ingredients and have them at the ready for a dish that's going to come together very quickly. We mostly serve this particular dish with quick-cooking thin Chinese noodles because it often takes longer to cook rice than it does to prepare the beef and sauce. You can't get many weekday meals faster than that.

1. Season the steak strips with salt and pepper, and heat 3 tbsp peanut oil in a very hot wok.

2. Quickly stir fry the steak for only 1-2 minutes. Be careful not to overcook the beef at this stage. Remove beef from the wok and set aside.

3. Add another 2 tbsp of peanut oil to the wok and quickly sauté the minced garlic for only a few seconds.

4. Add all of the remaining ingredients to the wok except the cornstarch slurry and bell pepper.

5. Simmer the sauce for about 5 minutes then stir in the cornstarch slurry, stirring constantly until it thickens to the consistency of a glaze.

6. Toss the beef back into the sauce along with one chopped red bell pepper and cook only enough to heat through, about 1 minute.

7. Serve immediately over rice or Chinese noodles and garnish with toasted sesame seeds and/or green onion.

Creamy Lemon Pepper Scallops Linguine

PREP TIME: **15** MINUTES | COOK TIME: **15** MINUTES | SERVES **4**

¾ lb dry linguine pasta

reserve up to 1 cup of pasta water

12 large scallops

salt and pepper to season

2 tbsp canola oil

3 tbsp olive oil

3 cloves garlic, chopped

1½ cups fish stock (you can substitute chicken or vegetable stock)

½ cup dry white wine

½ to 1 tsp freshly ground black pepper, according to taste

pinch of salt

zest of 1 large lemon, finely grated

juice of 1 large lemon (zest before juicing)

1 tsp finely chopped fresh dill

½ cup whipping cream

This creamy pasta dish with the bright, tangy flavour of lemon with spicy pepper probably isn't as indulgent as you might think. There's only a half cup of cream added to the sauce, which for 4 servings equals only two tablespoons per person. The secret here is well known in Italian cooking, where a little of the water from cooking the pasta is reserved to add while combining the linguine and sauce over low heat. This action takes advantage of the starch at the surface of the pasta, which helps to thicken the sauce just slightly and coat the pasta beautifully.

This quick and easy dish is a perfect choice for a mid-week celebration dinner when you don't have much time. I love small pasta portions as an appetizer course at a special dinner, and this one is perfect when served with just a single large seared scallop on top. Choose the rest of your menu carefully, though, because expectations will be set pretty high with this as a starter course!

1. Cook the linguine in salted water to al dente, about 8-10 minutes or as directed. It's important not to overcook the linguine. Drain and reserve up to a cup of the pasta water.

2. While the linguine is cooking, lightly season the scallops with salt and pepper on both sides and pan sear them in the canola oil in a hot sauté pan over medium-high heat. Large scallops should take no more than a couple of minutes per side, depending on their size. Make sure they have good golden colour. Remove from heat and set aside while you prepare the sauce.

3. In a large sauté pan, heat the olive oil over medium heat and add the garlic. Cook for only a minute to soften the garlic slightly.

4. Add the fish stock, wine, black pepper, and pinch of salt. Simmer until the volume of the liquid reduces by about half.

5. Add the lemon zest, lemon juice, dill, and whipping cream and simmer for another 2 or 3 minutes before adding the pasta. Let the pasta simmer in the sauce, tossing it with tongs as the sauce reduces and coats the pasta. If need be, add some of the reserved pasta water to the pan a little at a time while you toss the pasta in the sauce. In the final minute or so, add the scallops to bring them back up to heat before serving. Serve with chopped dill and a little grated lemon zest as garnishes.

Thirty Minute Easy Chicken
and Chickpea Curry

PREP TIME: **10** MINUTES | COOK TIME: **20** MINUTES | SERVES **4**

This recipe was the result of a challenge I set for myself based on an email I received from a reader of my blog. She asked if I had a really quick chicken curry recipe that didn't use a lot of hard-to-find spices, was only mildly spicy and low in fat. This is what I came up with to meet those criteria.

Long story short, even with only a few ingredients and spices, it was terrific. Spouse is not one for hot curries, so she was particularly pleased with this dish; it's her new favourite. The kids scarfed theirs down too and were even happy to have the leftovers the next day. I would absolutely recommend making a double batch and plan for leftovers of this tasty, economical meal.

1½ lb boneless, skinless chicken breasts or thighs, diced

salt and pepper to season

3 tbsp peanut oil (or vegetable oil)

4 cloves garlic, minced

1 medium onion, diced fine

2 tsp turmeric

2 tbsp yellow curry powder

2 tsp garam masala

½ tsp ground cardamom

2 tbsp grated fresh ginger

1½ cups chicken stock

1 cup drained low-fat yogurt (or low-fat Greek yogurt)

2 cups (drained and rinsed) canned chick peas

1. Season the diced chicken pieces with salt and pepper.

2. Heat the peanut oil in a large heavy bottomed Dutch oven over medium-high heat. Brown the chicken pieces for a few minutes.

3. Remove the chicken from the pot and add the garlic and onions. Cook them for a few minutes until they soften then add the turmeric, yellow curry powder, garam masala, and cardamom. Stir them well into the onions and garlic and cook for two minutes, stirring constantly.

4. Return the browned chicken to the pot along with the fresh ginger and chicken stock. Cover and bring to a slow simmer for 10 minutes.

5. Add the yogurt and chickpeas and simmer slowly for an additional 5-10 minutes.

6. Serve over plain basmati rice.

Mediterranean Lemon Butter Chicken

PREP TIME: **10** MINUTES | COOK TIME: **20** MINUTES | SERVES **4**

Boneless chicken breasts are always a great choice for quick and easy meals, but they are particularly quick in this recipe. They're either pounded thin or sliced to half their thickness before quick frying for a really speedy meal.

The rich and buttery sauce is tempered by the slight saltiness of feta cheese and sun-dried olives and brightened by the fresh herbs and tangy lemon. Just delicious! I love Kalamata olives that are naturally sun-dried and packed in oil for this recipe, but some people find them quite intensely flavoured. Feel free to substitute other black olives if you prefer; there will still be plenty of flavour on the plate.

4 large boneless chicken breasts, pounded to ½-inch thickness or split horizontally

salt and pepper to season

3 tbsp + 3 tbsp olive oil

2 cloves garlic, minced

½ cup chicken stock

½ cup dry white wine

⅓ cup sun-dried Kalamata olives

2 tbsp capers

2 tsp black pepper

juice and zest of 1 large lemon

2 tbsp chopped fresh oregano

2 tbsp chopped fresh chives

4 tbsp butter

⅓ cup crumbled feta cheese

1. Season the chicken breasts with salt and pepper and quick fry in 3 tbsp olive oil in a sauté pan over medium-high heat for about 3 minutes per side until cooked but still juicy. Remove from the pan and hold in a warm oven.

2. In the same sauté pan, add 3 tbsp of olive oil and the minced garlic for 1 minute until the garlic softens.

3. Add the chicken stock and white wine. Simmer for a few minutes until the volume decreases by about half.

4. Add the chicken back to the pan along with all the other ingredients except the feta cheese.

5. Toss together until the butter has melted and the chicken is warmed through. At the last minute, toss in the feta cheese.

6. Serve over cooked pasta.

Low-Fat Ranch Chicken Salad

PREP TIME: **15** MINUTES + REFRIGERATION TIME | SERVES **4–6**

1 cup low-fat or fat-free yogurt

1 clove garlic, very well minced

1 tbsp very finely chopped basil

1 tbsp finely chopped fresh dill

3 tbsp apple cider vinegar

1 tbsp Worcestershire sauce

1 tbsp Dijon mustard

½ tbsp honey

pinch kosher salt

½ tsp freshly ground
black pepper

3 tbsp minced green onion

3–4 cups diced cooked chicken

½ cup finely diced celery

½ cup finely diced red
bell peppers

The dressing for this tasty chicken salad is a homemade version using fat-free yogurt. Simple ingredients like garlic and Dijon mustard that you probably already have in your fridge get added to the yogurt to create a fat-free dressing which then gets tossed with some diced chicken breast, peppers, and celery to create a delicious chicken salad. That chicken salad can make some fantastic sandwiches for lunch or as the base for a terrific lunch or dinner salad. It certainly is an excellent way to use that leftover chicken from Sunday dinner.

1.   Mix together the first 11 ingredients and let sit in the fridge for several hours or overnight for the flavour to fully develop.

2.   Add the diced chicken, celery, and bell peppers, and toss well.

3.   Serve on sandwiches or as a delicious addition to a mixed garden salad for a complete meal.

tip > Strain 2 cups of yogurt for several hours in a colander lined with coffee filters and use the resulting thick yogurt in step 1 of this recipe as a delicious dip for vegetables or a spread for crackers or crusty bread—a terrific party food idea.

DRY-RUBBED CHICKEN

4 large boneless, skinless chicken breasts

1 tbsp smoked paprika

¼ tsp chipotle powder

1 tbsp powdered ginger

1 tbsp dry mustard

½ tsp dry thyme

½ tsp black pepper

1½ tsp garlic powder

1 tsp salt

1 tbsp brown sugar

1 tsp chili powder

LEMON DIJON SALAD DRESSING

⅓ cup olive oil

juice and finely minced zest of 1 lemon

3 tbsp Dijon mustard

pinch of salt

pinch of pepper

1½ tbsp honey

SPINACH, PINEAPPLE, AND POMEGRANATE SALAD

6 cups (approx.) baby spinach or mixed baby greens

½ cup sliced radishes

1 cup julienne sweet bell peppers

½ English cucumber, sliced

seeds of half a pomegranate

1½ cups lightly grilled diced golden pineapple

Smoked Chicken, Spinach, Grilled Pineapple, and Pomegranate Salad

PREP TIME: **10** MINUTES | COOK TIME: **1** HOUR

SERVES **4**

I do love a colourful, flavourful dinner salad, and this one is a particularly delicious example. The chicken breasts are dry rubbed with smoky spices and then slowly open roasted on a rack in the oven (or under indirect low heat on a backyard gas grill). This provides delicious juicy chicken chunks to enjoy with the spinach and other vegetables and, of course, the sweet grilled pineapple and tangy pomegranate seeds. A simple homemade lemon Dijon dressing completes this balanced, nutritious, colourful, flavourful, and oh-so-satisfying dinner salad.

DRY-RUBBED CHICKEN

1.　Wash the chicken breasts and pat dry with paper towels.

2.　Combine the remaining ingredients to create the dry rub and sprinkle it on both sides of the chicken breasts. If you don't use all the rub, just save it in an airtight container for next time. Don't save any dry rub that comes into contact with the chicken though. Use a spoon to sprinkle on the rub so that you do not cross contaminate it.

3.　At this point, you can grill the chicken or place the chicken breasts on a rack in a roasting pan and roast at only 275°F for about 1 hour, depending on the size of the chicken breasts. Always use a meat thermometer inserted into the middle of the thickest part of the chicken breast until the temperature reaches 170°F. Let the chicken rest for 10 minutes before dicing and adding to the salad.

LEMON DIJON SALAD DRESSING

1. Simply shake all of the ingredients together in an airtight container until well combined.

SPINACH, PINEAPPLE, AND POMEGRANATE SALAD

1. Toss all the ingredients and serve topped with the cooked chicken and lemon Dijon dressing.

MANGO LIME SALSA

1 large mango, peeled and diced small

1 clove garlic, minced

juice of 1 lime

zest of 1 lime, finely chopped

½ red onion, diced

1 tbsp finely chopped jalapeño pepper

1 tsp salt

½ tsp coarse ground black pepper

1 tsp ground cumin

1 tbsp brown sugar

¼ cup chopped fresh cilantro

½ red bell pepper, diced small

TACO BOWLS

4 whole-wheat, seven-inch tortillas

About 2 tsp olive oil

TACO SEASONING

2 tbsp chili powder

1 tbsp paprika (or smoked paprika)

2 tsp ground cumin

1 tsp dry oregano

½ tsp cinnamon

½ tsp chili flakes
(or more for a spicier seasoning)

CHICKEN TACO SALAD

2 tbsp olive oil

4 boneless, skinless chicken breasts,
cut in ½-inch cubes

2 cloves garlic, minced

salt and pepper

taco seasoning

3 cups (approx.) shredded romaine lettuce

1 small red bell pepper, sliced

2 tomatoes, diced

½ cup black olives

1 cup cooked kidney beans (optional)

Low-Fat Chicken Taco Salad *with* Mango Salsa

PREP TIME: **10** MINUTES + STANDING TIME
COOK TIME: **20** MINUTES | SERVES **4**

In this low-fat chicken taco salad, a baked whole-wheat taco bowl gets filled with seasoned chicken breast and plenty of vegetables before being topped with a mango lime salsa, which serves as a fat-free dressing. It's too delicious to even think about how healthy this is.

MANGO LIME SALSA

1. Toss all ingredients together well in a glass bowl.

2. Let stand for about 2 hours before serving, stirring occasionally.

TACO BOWLS

1. Preheat oven to 300°F.

2. Very lightly brush or spray both sides of the tortillas with olive oil and fit into small, oven-safe, cereal-sized bowls. 16-oz baking ramekins are also ideal.

3. Bake for about 15-20 minutes until crisp.

TACO SEASONING

1. Mix all of the seasoning ingredients together and set aside before preparing the chicken taco salad.

CHICKEN TACO SALAD

1. In a large skillet, heat the 2 tbsp olive oil then add the cubed chicken breasts and garlic.

2. Season the chicken with salt and pepper and cook it just until lightly browned.

3. In the last minute of cooking, add the Taco Seasoning to the chicken, tossing well to coat all the pieces in the seasoning mix.

4. Add the salad ingredients to the baked taco bowls, then top with the cooked chicken and the mango salsa to serve.

Cherry Orange Pork Medallions

PREP TIME: **10** MINUTES | COOK TIME: **20** MINUTES | SERVES **4–6**

Here's a sweet-and-sour cherry sauce with a citrus twist that goes deliciously well with simple pan-rushed pork tenderloin that's sliced in thin medallions. It's wonderful when cherries are in season, but frozen cherries are just as good in a recipe you can make all year round. It's an easy, fast but impressive dinner to serve guests, especially when you get the pork cooked perfectly. They won't believe you spent so little time preparing it.

PORK MEDALLIONS

3 tbsp olive oil

2 lb pork tenderloin

salt and pepper to season

CHERRY ORANGE SAUCE

2 tbsp olive oil

2 cloves garlic, minced

2 cups chopped cherries, fresh or frozen

½ tsp grated orange zest

1 cup orange juice

¼ tsp cracked black pepper

3 tbsp honey

1 tbsp apple cider vinegar

salt to season

¼ tsp of cinnamon

½ tsp ground ginger (or 1 tsp fresh grated ginger)

1 rounded tsp cornstarch

1–2 oz water

PORK MEDALLIONS

1. Preheat oven to 375°F.

2. Heat the olive oil in a cast-iron skillet. Season the pork tenderloin with salt and pepper and quickly brown it on all sides in the hot pan.

3. Place the hot pan in the oven and roast the pork for 15-20 minutes, depending on the thickness of the tenderloin. Use a meat thermometer to get a reading of 160°F at the thickest part of the meat then remove from the oven and let the meat rest for 10 minutes before thinly slicing and serving with the cherry orange sauce.

CHERRY ORANGE SAUCE

1. Over medium-low heat, add the oil and garlic to a small saucepan. Cook only for a couple of minutes before adding all the other ingredients, except the cornstarch and water.

2. Simmer together until the volume is reduced by about ¼.

3. Stir the cornstarch and water together and add to the simmering sauce. Stir constantly as it thickens. Cook for only a minute or so more before serving with the sliced pork.

Mediterranean Lemon Chicken Orzo Salad

PREP TIME: **20** MINUTES | COOK TIME: **10** MINUTES | SERVES **4**

At our house, this is one of our favourite Leftover Rescue Recipes, especially after a roast-chicken dinner on the weekend. It's an ideal Monday meal if you're using leftover chicken, but it's also well worth grilling or baking some boneless chicken breasts for the sole purpose of making this delicious salad. You may even want to roast an extra chicken for Sunday dinner, just with this tasty dinner in mind.

1 cup orzo (whole wheat if you can find it)

6-inch piece cucumber, seeded and diced

½ cup diced red bell pepper

1 small red onion, diced small

juice and finely minced zest of 1 lemon

½ cup chopped olives

½ cup diced feta

4 tbsp chopped fresh oregano (or leave the leaves whole if you like)

½ tsp cracked black pepper

¼ cup extra-virgin olive oil

1½ cups leftover diced chicken or diced grilled chicken breast

1. Cook the orzo in salted water until cooked but firm, usually under 10 minutes. Don't overcook and get mushy orzo; al dente pasta is a must in this recipe.

2. When cooked, rinse the orzo with cold water in a colander and let drain completely for several minutes.

3. Add all of the remaining ingredients and toss together until well combined.

4. Refrigerate until ready to serve. This salad is generally best when prepared an hour or two in advance.

Low-Fat Turkey Sausage *and* Brown Rice

PREP TIME: **15** MINUTES | COOK TIME: **25** MINUTES | SERVES **4–6**

1 lb low-fat turkey sausage meat

2 tbsp olive oil

3 cloves garlic, minced

1 medium red onion, finely diced

2 stalks celery, finely chopped

1 carrot, finely diced

1 red bell pepper, diced

½ tsp salt

½ tsp freshly ground black pepper

1 tsp cumin

1½ tbsp chili

1 tbsp chipotle powder

2 tbsp smoked paprika

3 cups canned diced tomatoes

1 tbsp Scotch bonnet sauce
or hot sauce (optional)

2 cups low-sodium vegetable
or chicken broth

1 cup brown rice

garnish of fresh cilantro,
chopped

As a terrific weekday meal, this recipe ticks all the right boxes. It's quick, easy, nutritious, delicious, and economical. You can use whatever low-fat sausage you like, but in this version I've chosen a low-fat turkey Italian variety that adds lots of flavour to the dish. The recipe is little more than stir frying the sausage, chopping the vegetables, and throwing all the ingredients in one pot to simmer for 15-20 minutes until the rice is cooked. And the spices in this dish can easily be adjusted, so please feel free to cut the spice amounts down to suit your taste. Or ramp up the heat if that's how you like it.

1. In a covered wok or a Dutch oven, brown the sausage in the olive oil.

2. Add the garlic and onions and stir-fry for a couple of minutes until the onions begin to soften. Add all of the other ingredients except for the rice and fresh cilantro and bring to a boil.

3. Add the rice and turn the heat down to a slow simmer. Cover and cook for 15-20 minutes until the rice is tender.

4. Serve with a sprinkle of chopped fresh cilantro.

White Bean Chicken Chili

PREP TIME: **15** MINUTES | COOK TIME: **45** MINUTES | SERVES **4**

3 tbsp olive oil

4 boneless, skinless chicken breasts (or 8 boneless, skinless chicken thighs), cut into 2-inch chunks

salt and pepper to season

4 medium carrots, chopped

1 large leek, chopped

3 cloves garlic, minced

1 white onion, chopped

2½ cups cooked white kidney beans (any white bean can be substituted)

2 cups baby corn

3–4 cups chicken stock

1 tsp ground cumin

1 tsp ground thyme

1½ tbsp chili powder

salt and pepper to taste

juice of 1 lime

garnish of freshly chopped cilantro

Somewhere between a soup and a stew, this healthy white bean chicken chili is a meal that totally satisfies. Chili powder and cumin are familiar flavours here, and the white beans make it a complete, hearty, but healthy meal. Some great cornbread would be fantastic on the side.

1. In a large pot or Dutch oven over medium-high heat, add the olive oil and chicken chunks.

2. Season the chicken with salt and pepper and brown quickly before removing the chicken from the pan and setting aside.

3. To the pan add the carrots, leeks, garlic, and onion.

4. Sauté over medium heat until the onions and leeks have softened. Add the chicken back to the pot along with the white kidney beans, baby corn, chicken stock, cumin, thyme, chili powder, salt and pepper.

5. Simmer gently for 30 minutes. Just before serving, add the juice of 1 lime and garnish with freshly chopped cilantro.

Orange Mint Grilled Shrimp

PREP TIME: **30** MINUTES | COOK TIME: **6** MINUTES | SERVES **2–4**

You might think that the combination of orange and mint is a little weird, and the first time I experimented with it, I was a little skeptical too. But I found myself making these orange mint grilled shrimp again and again. We now often serve them at weekend barbeques as an appetizer. When served on a mixed green salad with fresh mint leaves and orange sections, it also makes a perfect light summer lunch dish.

note > This recipe also works well on a well-heated cast-iron grill pan.

⅓ cup orange juice

zest of 1 orange, finely chopped

3 tbsp chopped fresh mint

2 tbsp olive oil

1 clove garlic, finely minced

1 tbsp honey

pinch salt

pinch black pepper

1 lb fresh shrimp, peeled and de-veined

3–4 bamboo skewers

1. Whisk together the first 8 ingredients to make the marinade.

2. Marinate the shrimp in the marinade for no longer than 20 minutes; longer than this can allow the citric acid in the orange juice to break down the surface of the shrimp and dry them out when cooked.

3. While the shrimp are marinating you can also soak 3 or 4 bamboo skewers in water to prepare them for the grill.

4. Push the shrimp onto the pre-soaked bamboo skewers. If you like, you can alternate the shrimp with pieces of sweet bell peppers and/or red onions.

5. Place the shrimp skewers onto a preheated grill on medium heat and grill for only 2-3 minutes per side depending on the size of shrimp that you are using. These are delicious served as an appetizer for 4 or with an orange, mint, and mixed green salad as a main course for two.

Parmesan Bacon Chicken Linguine

PREP TIME: **20** MINUTES | COOK TIME: **20** MINUTES | SERVES **4**

This recipe was inspired by a reader who emailed me to ask if I had an egg-less recipe for pasta carbonara with chicken? The classic recipe uses basic ingredients like pasta, garlic, pancetta, Parmesan, and pepper but the sauce is egg based, which the reader could not eat. I suggested an alternative using cream and chicken stock. I tried it that evening myself and the kids loved it, so we've made it several times since at our house too.

¾ lb dry linguine

6 slices crisp-cooked bacon, chopped. Reserve a little for garnishing the plates

4 small boneless, skinless chicken breasts, cubed

salt and pepper to season

3 tbsp olive oil

6 cloves garlic, minced

1½ cups low-sodium or salt-free chicken stock

¾ cup whipping cream

½ cup red bell pepper, diced small (optional)

½ cup grated Parmesan cheese

2 tbsp chopped fresh herbs for garnish (optional)

1. Cook the dry linguine to al dente in salted water and drain.

2. Crisp cook the bacon in a large sauté pan and roughly chop it. Set aside.

3. Cut the chicken breasts into bite-sized cubes, lightly season with salt and pepper, and pan fry them in the bacon fat for only a few minutes until fully cooked. Remove the chicken from the pan and set aside with the bacon.

4. Drain the bacon fat from the pan and add the olive oil and garlic; cook for only a minute to slightly soften the garlic.

5. Add the chicken stock and simmer quickly for a few minutes until the liquid has reduced by about ⅓. Add the cream and simmer for an additional 2 minutes.

6. Season with salt and pepper if needed, then add the bacon, bell pepper and the chicken to the sauce. Simmer for only 1-2 minutes to warm the chicken through before adding the cooked pasta and Parmesan cheese.

7. Toss together the pasta and sauce very well while still on the heat until the sauce thickens to the consistency you like.

8. Garnish with some reserved chopped bacon, extra Parmesan cheese, and a sprinkle of fresh herbs before serving.

tip > When making pasta that is simmered and tossed for a short time in its sauce, like this recipe, I sometimes prepare the sauce in a wok. The bottom part of the wok is small enough to simmer a sauce and the widening upper level leaves plenty of room to easily toss cooked pasta, ensuring an even coating of sauce throughout.

In many ways, I see this section of my cookbooks as maybe being the most important. The hustle and bustle of the work and school week can occasionally overwhelm even the most organized person, and family mealtime often suffers as a result. Weekend days then become even more important because that's when we get a chance to slow down with family and friends and enjoy a home-cooked meal that's meant to be prepared and enjoyed at a more leisurely pace. These comfort-food meals are meant to help press that pause button and bring everyone back to the table with dishes that are destined to be new family favourites.

slow-cooked sunday

Italian Sausage *and* Chicken Cassoulet 114

Braised Beef Pot Pie *with* Biscuit Topping 116

Tomato Fennel Braised Chicken Thighs 118

Moroccan Meatball Stew 120

Asian Spice Brined Roast Chicken 122

Brown Sugar Pecan Glazed Pork Loin 124

Sage Thyme Chicken Stew *with* Cornbread Dumplings 126

Burgundy Thyme Pot Roast 128

Foolproof Dry-Rubbed Oven Ribs 130

Honey Barbecue Pulled Beef Sandwiches *with* Creamy Dijon Coleslaw 132

Easy Lemon Dijon Roasted Chicken 134

Dijon Beef and Mushroom Pie 136

Italian Sausage *and* Chicken Cassoulet

PREP TIME: **30** MINUTES | COOK TIME: **2** HOURS | SERVES **4–6**

2 or 3 chicken legs

pinch salt and pepper to season

canola oil for frying

1 lb good-quality Italian sausage (mild or hot, your choice)

3 large shallots, finely diced

6 cloves garlic, minced

1 small red onion, finely diced

3 stalks celery, finely diced

1½ cups low-sodium or salt-free chicken stock

2 or 3 large tomatoes, finely diced

4 large carrots, cut in 3-inch sticks

2 cups canned Roma beans, rinsed

1½ tsp dried oregano (or 2 tbsp fresh chopped oregano)

1 tsp dried thyme (or 3 springs fresh thyme)

3 bay leaves

½ tsp salt

½ tsp freshly ground black pepper

I've given this classic French comfort-food dish a little bit of an Italian twist here using Italian sausage and Roma beans. The broth in this dish gets so deeply rich and flavourful in the slow-cooking process, it really is incredible. This is a dish that can be doubled or even tripled to feed a large group easily, and if you follow the serving tip suggested, you could stretch it even further. I just love meals like this because they are examples of simple cooking that yields extraordinary results.

1. Preheat oven to 325°F.

2. Season the chicken legs on both sides with salt and pepper.

3. Add a little canola oil to a cast-iron pan over medium-high heat and brown the chicken legs and sausages on all sides, then set them aside.

4. Reduce the heat to medium and add the shallots, garlic, red onion, and celery to the pan. Lightly season with salt and pepper and cook until the onions have softened but not browned.

5. Transfer the cooked shallots, garlic, red onion, and celery to a large covered Dutch oven or roasting pan. Add the chicken stock, diced tomatoes, carrots, Roma beans, oregano, thyme, bay leaves, salt, and pepper. Stir together gently and add the sausages and chicken legs on top of the beans and vegetables.

6. Cover and cook in the oven for 2-2½ hours or until the chicken is tender enough to fall off the bone.

7. Serve the chicken pieces and sausages on top of the Roma beans and vegetables.

Braised Beef Pot Pie *with* Biscuit Topping

PREP TIME: **20** MINUTES | COOK TIME: **3** HOURS | SERVES **6**

BRAISED BEEF

2½–3 lb beef pot roast (blade or chuck roast work well)

salt and pepper to season

½ cup flour to dredge the beef cubes

3–4 tbsp vegetable oil

2 large onions, diced

4 cloves garlic, minced

4 tbsp butter

6 cups low-sodium beef stock (you can replace 2 cups of stock with an equal amount of stout beer or red wine for an extra rich gravy)

1½ tbsp dried thyme

½ tsp ground nutmeg

½ tsp salt

1 tsp coarsely ground black pepper

2 bay leaves

½ cup orange juice

BUTTERMILK BISCUITS

2 cups all-purpose flour

3 tsp baking powder

¼ tsp baking soda

¼ cup + 1 tbsp very cold salted butter, cut in small cubes

1 cup buttermilk

Classic pot pies can be quite time consuming, so it's nice to have another comfort food alternative to turn to that doesn't take as much effort as making pastry for a top and bottom crust pie. The shortcut in our house is most often some quickly prepared buttermilk biscuits, which get baked on the beef filling after it has been braised to tender perfection for a few hours. If you're looking to boost the flavour of this biscuit topping even more, add some chopped fresh herbs like chives or oregano to the biscuits or even a little grated Parmesan or white cheddar cheese.

You can of course add vegetables or mushrooms to the stewed beef in the last hour or so of braising, but I most often like to serve it with mashed or roasted potatoes and vegetables on the side.

BRAISED BEEF

1. Preheat oven to 300°F.

2. Trim the beef roast of excess fat then cut it into 1½-inch cubes.

3. Season the cubes with salt and pepper then roll them in the plain flour to coat them well.

4. In a cast-iron skillet, heat the oil over medium-high heat and brown the beef cubes well in small batches. Do not crowd the pan with the beef or it will be harder to brown and drier when cooked.

5. Transfer the browned beef to a covered roasting pan or Dutch oven.

6. Melt the butter in sauté pan and add the onions and garlic. Sauté over medium heat until the onions have softened, but not browned, then add them to the roasting pan with the beef.

7. Add the beef stock, thyme, nutmeg, salt, pepper, bay leaves, and orange juice.

8. Stir and cover the roasting pan tightly with aluminum foil before adding the lid.

9. Bake in the oven for 2½-3 hours or until the beef is fall-apart tender.

10. Remove the cover and add the prepared biscuits to the top of the beef and gravy.

11. Increase the heat to 375°F and bake until the biscuits are baked through and golden brown on top.

BUTTERMILK BISCUITS

1. In a food processor, blend together the flour, baking powder, and baking soda.

2. Pulse in the cold butter. Do not over incorporate the butter into the flour. Similar to making a flaky pastry, small pieces of butter should be visible in the flour.

3. Transfer this mixture from the food processor into a large mixing bowl and make a well in the center. Pour in the buttermilk.

4. Working very quickly with a wooden spoon, fold the dry mixture through the buttermilk, only until the flour disappears, then stop immediately.

5. Drop the sticky dough onto a well-floured countertop or bread board. Sprinkle the top of the dough with additional flour as well and flour your hands to handle the dough. I don't even use a rolling pin for these biscuits; the dough is soft enough to pat it out gently with floured hands to a thickness of about 1½ inches.

6. Using a sharp 3- to 4-inch biscuit cutter, cut the biscuits out and place them on top of the beef and gravy to bake as instructed above.

7. You can use a smaller biscuit cutter if you like, but the baking time will be about 5 minutes less.

Tomato Fennel Braised Chicken Thighs

PREP TIME: **15** MINUTES | COOK TIME: **2** HOURS | SERVES **4–6**

4 tbsp olive oil

2–3 lb boneless, skinless chicken thighs

salt and pepper to season

flour for dredging

2 cups chicken stock

6 large ripe tomatoes, diced (or 3½ cups diced canned tomatoes)

½ large bulb fennel (or 1 small bulb), diced small

4 cloves garlic, minced

1 large red onion, diced

1 tbsp dried oregano

¼ tsp chili flakes (optional)

1½ tbsp brown sugar

½ tsp salt

½ tsp freshly ground black pepper

I love the flavour boost that fennel gives to a great tomato sauce, and when you slowly braise chicken thighs in that sauce to tender deliciousness, it just gets even better. Although this recipe is slow cooked for up to a couple of hours, the preparation is quite fast and fuss free. Other than browning the chicken thighs in a skillet, the only other work is chopping the tomatoes, garlic, fennel, and onions to be added to the braising pan. These vegetables then cook to tender during the braising time. And with a quick blitz in the food process or, as I do, in the pan with an immersion blender, they are transformed into a delicious sauce.

1. Preheat oven to 300°F.

2. Heat olive oil in a large skillet over medium heat.

3. Season chicken thighs with salt and pepper and then dredge them in plain flour.

4. Brown the chicken thighs on both sides.

5. Deglaze the pan with the chicken stock, making sure to loosen any browned bits from the bottom of the pan.

6. In a covered roasting pan, toss together the remaining ingredients.

7. Add the browned chicken thighs on top of the vegetables and pour the chicken stock over everything.

8. Cover and roast for about 1½-2 hours or until most of the liquid has cooked off and the chicken is tender and falling apart.

9. To serve, you can either spoon the vegetables over rice or pasta or, if you prefer, process them slightly in a food processor (or in the pan with an immersion blender) to make a sauce as is shown in the photo.

½ cup bread crumbs

¼ cup milk

2 lb ground lamb (or beef)

1 tsp dry oregano

¼ tsp ground nutmeg

1 beaten egg

½ tsp salt

½ tsp black pepper

2 tbsp Worcestershire sauce

a little olive oil for frying the
meatballs

1 carrot, diced carrot

1 stalk celery, diced

4 cloves garlic, chopped

1 red onion, diced

6 cups diced canned tomatoes

¾ cup currants

½ cup raisins

3 bay leaves

1 tsp ground coriander

1 tsp ground cardamom

1 tsp turmeric

2 tsp ground cumin

4 tsp ground cinnamon

¼ tsp ground cloves

½ tsp ground nutmeg

1 small red chili, minced
(or 1 tbsp chili paste)

2 tbsp brown sugar

salt and pepper to season

2 cups cooked or canned
chickpeas, rinsed

1 cup olives (optional)

Moroccan Meatball Stew

PREP TIME: **15** MINUTES | COOK TIME: **2** HOURS
SERVES **4–6**

Here's a terrific weekend slow-cooked supper that will fill the entire house with the most amazing fragrance of spices. It really is a glorious, layered combination of flavours from the sweet currants and raisins to the salty olives, with just the right amount of gentle spicy heat. This recipe is also ideal for the slow cooker. Just add the chickpeas along with the other ingredients as the only modification to the recipe. Leave the olives until the very end just to warm them, or the stew may be too salty. The depth of flavour in this dish, plus the heavenly scent while it slowly cooks, makes it a real feast for the senses.

1. Soak the bread crumbs in the milk for 10 minutes.

2. Add the ground lamb (or beef), the oregano, nutmeg, beaten egg, salt, pepper, and Worcestershire sauce.

3. Mix well and form into 1½-inch balls. Fry the meatballs in olive oil to brown on all sides. Remove meatballs to a covered, oven-safe casserole dish or small roasting pan.

4. Preheat oven to 350°F.

5. Add the diced carrot, celery, garlic, and red onion to the pan after the meatballs are browned. Sauté together until the onions soften and then add this mixture to the pan with the meatballs along with the next 14 ingredients (everything except the chickpeas and olives).

6. Bake, covered, for about 1 hour and then remove from the oven.

7. Reduce the oven heat to 325°F and add the chickpeas to the stew. Return to the oven for 1 hour. In the last 10 minutes of cooking time, you can add the olives if you are using them.

8. Serve over couscous.

Asian Spice Brined Roast Chicken

PREP TIME: **30** MINUTES + BRINING TIME | COOK TIME: **1** HOUR **30** MINUTES | SERVES **4–6**

Sunday dinner is still a big deal in our family, and what better for the occasion than a perfectly roasted chicken? Isn't this one a beauty?

Beside the fact that brining poultry adds deep-seasoned flavour and ensures succulent, juicy meat, I also love the way it allows for an evenly cooked skin. I think the extra moisture in the skin of the brined roast chicken takes more time to brown, and when it does, it does so more evenly. I mean, look at that chicken! It looks like it popped out of a Norman Rockwell painting.

The brining process is the absolute best way to add flavour to the meat as well. Herbs, spices, onion, shallots, garlic, and citrus are all great choices to add to the brining mix. In this recipe, I decided to experiment with some Asian-inspired spice flavours, and it was absolutely delicious.

1 small red onion or 1 large shallot, sliced thinly

4 cloves garlic, minced

1 tbsp black peppercorns

2 tbsp Szechuan peppers (or 2 dried red chilies)

2 tbsp fennel seeds

4 star anise

2 tbsp cardamom pods

about 8 cups cold water (only enough to cover the chicken)

⅓ cup brown sugar

⅓ cup kosher salt

¼ cup soy sauce

one 4–5 lb roasting chicken

1. Add the onion, garlic, peppercorns, Szechuan peppers, fennel seeds, star anise, and cardamom pods to a small pot of boiling water (1-2 cups) and remove from the heat. Allow to steep, off the heat, for 5-10 minutes.

2. Add the brown sugar, salt, and soy sauce to 6 cups cold water and stir until the salt and sugar are completely dissolved.

3. Add the steeped spice mixture to the cold water and stir.

4. Submerge the chicken in the brining liquid, cover, and place in the fridge for 8-24 hours.

5. Remove chicken from the brine and discard the liquid.

6. Pat the chicken dry with paper towels and, if time allows, let it sit in the fridge uncovered for a couple of hours.

7. Preheat oven to 350°F.

8. Truss the chicken as you wish or just fold the wing tips underneath and tie the legs together with some butcher string.

9. Place on a roasting rack and roast **uncovered** for about 20 minutes per pound. The cooking time is approximate. Always use a meat thermometer to ensure the internal temperature at the thickest parts of the breast and thigh are at least 185-190°F.

10. It is very important to let the chicken rest when it comes out of the oven for at least 10-15 minutes. This allows the juices to settle back into the meat and it will be moister when carved.

tips for brining poultry >

1. Don't choose too large a container. Use one large enough to submerge the chicken but not much larger. This will ensure your herbs, spices, and other flavour elements stay concentrated and more intensely flavour the chicken.

2. When using fresh herbs, chop them finely to extract as much flavour as possible.

3. When using dried spices or herbs, like in this recipe, steep them for 5-10 minutes in a cup or two of boiling water before adding to the rest of the brining liquid.

4. Don't fear that you're using too much salt and reduce the amount. The vast majority of the salt will get thrown out with the brining liquid; it only seems like a larger amount because of the need to dissolve it in a large volume of water.

5. For perfectly browned chicken skin, dry it well with paper towels after it comes out of the brining liquid and let the chicken stand uncovered in the fridge for several hours, if you can, for the surface of the skin to dry out a little. This ensures the outermost surface skin will seal faster in the oven, which will not only aid in browning but keep the meat moister as it roasts.

Brown Sugar Pecan Glazed Pork Loin

PREP TIME: **15** MINUTES | COOK TIME: **1** HOUR **30** MINUTES | SERVES **8–10**

3½ lb pork-loin roast

1 tsp salt

½ tsp freshly ground black pepper

¾ cup light brown sugar

¼ cup Dijon mustard

¾ cup roughly chopped, unroasted pecans

The simple glaze we always use on baked ham at our house inspired this roast pork recipe. It's so simple and delicious that we rarely ever make ham without it. We also use the same glaze on roasted fresh pork as well, so when Spouse suggested a pecan-crusted version, I couldn't resist. It turned out to be one of the best roast pork dishes we've ever made, and we've made it many times since. The only secrets to this simple recipe are to keep basting the glaze over the meat and do not overcook the pork. A meat thermometer will always help you yield the best results with any kind of roast, including this juicy pork loin.

1. Preheat oven to 425°F.

2. Trim the fat from the roast, leaving only ¼-inch of fat on top at the most.

3. Season the pork loin with salt and pepper and open roast the pork on a parchment-lined cookie sheet in the oven for 30 minutes.

4. Combine the brown sugar and Dijon mustard into a paste and fold the chopped pecans into it.

5. Remove the roast from the oven after 30 minutes and reduce the heat to 375°F.

6. Spread the prepared paste evenly over the top of the roast and return to the oven.

7. Baste the roast about every 15 minutes, scooping up the glaze and nuts that fall off back over the top of the roast.

8. Continue to roast until the internal temperature of the roast hits 160°F on a meat thermometer.

9. Let the roast rest for 10 minutes after you take it out of the oven before carving and serving.

Sage Thyme Chicken Stew
with Cornbread Dumplings

PREP TIME: **20** MINUTES | COOK TIME: **2** HOURS **30** MINUTES | SERVES **4–6**

SAGE THYME CHICKEN STEW

3 tbsp olive oil

2½ lb boneless, skinless chicken breasts or thighs

pinch salt and pepper to season

3 cloves garlic, minced

1 large white onion, chopped

3 stalks celery, chopped

1 tbsp fresh thyme leaves

2 tbsp chopped fresh sage

2 cups + 3 cups chicken stock

4 carrots, sliced or cut in small chunks

1 cup corn kernels, fresh or frozen

½ cup peas, fresh or frozen

4 rounded tbsp flour

½ cup water

CORNBREAD DUMPLINGS

1 cup flour

½ cup yellow cornmeal

2 tbsp sugar

1½ tsp baking powder

⅓ cup cold butter

⅔ cup milk

This is one of my preferred snow-day meals to shake off the winter chill, but it's a great homey family meal at any time of the year when you need a little comfort-food love. This easy to make chicken stew is ready in only a couple of hours with fresh herb flavours to enhance the rich gravy. The cornbread dumplings are the perfect addition to this satisfying Sunday dinner meal. It's another fan favourite on *RockRecipes.com* and garners rave reviews like, "By far one of the best stew recipes I've ever tried!"

SAGE THYME CHICKEN STEW

1. Preheat oven to 350°F.

2. Over medium-high heat, add the olive oil to the bottom of a heavy-bottom Dutch oven. Add the chicken to the heated oil, season with salt and pepper, and cook for about 5 minutes, tossing often until the chicken has browned. Remove the chicken from the pot and set aside.

3. To the hot pot, add the garlic, onions, and celery and sauté until the onions soften. Return the chicken to the pot and add the thyme and sage. Add 2 cups of the chicken stock. The stock should be boiling hot to speed up the cooking time of this recipe. Stir together, cover, and cook in the oven for about 1 hour.

4. After an hour, add the carrots, corn, and peas along with the remaining 3 cups of hot chicken stock. Bring to a boil on the stove top and slowly add a thickening slurry made by whisking together the flour and water until no lumps are left; stir constantly as you add the slurry to the stew. Drop the cornbread dumpling batter in large rounded tablespoonfuls into the stew and return to the oven for 30 minutes before serving.

CORNBREAD DUMPLINGS

1. Sift together the flour, cornmeal, sugar, and baking powder. With a pastry blender or pulsing in a food processor, cut the butter into the flour until small pieces are still visible. Quickly stir in the milk with a wooden spoon until a thick batter forms.

Burgundy Thyme Pot Roast

PREP TIME: **30** MINUTES | COOK TIME: **3** HOURS | SERVES **4–6**

Can anything ever beat a great pot roast for Sunday dinner? This slow-cooked, tender pot roast is braised in red wine and onions, which produce a rich and very flavourful gravy. We love to serve this roast with Yorkshire pudding popovers and crispy roasted potatoes, the recipes for both of which can be found in the first *Rock Recipes* cookbook.

A fall-apart tender beef pot roast is one of the true joys of slow cooking, and this particular recipe is an exceptional example of how simple ingredients and preparation are all that's needed to create a home-cooked meal that's second to none.

4 lb blade roast (chuck roast)

2½–3 cups beef stock (if using store-bought stock, use salt-free or low-sodium brands)

1½ cups burgundy wine (any dry red wine can be substituted)

2 bay leaves

3 tbsp Worcestershire sauce

1 tsp freshly grated nutmeg

1 tsp black pepper

1 tsp kosher salt

6 springs fresh thyme (or 1 tbsp ground dry thyme)

3 cloves garlic, finely minced

1 lb carrots

1 lb parsnips

½ lb peeled small shallots or pearl onions

¼ cup all-purpose flour

1 cup warm water

1. Preheat oven to 325°F.

2. I like to make sure the roast is tied tightly with butcher string, which helps it hold together in the oven and makes it easier to remove and serve. Season the roast on all sides with salt and pepper.

3. Heat 3 tbsp vegetable oil in a cast-iron skillet over medium-high heat and brown the roast on all sides before transferring it to a covered roasting pan.

4. To the roasting pan add the beef stock, wine, bay leaves, Worcestershire sauce, nutmeg, pepper, kosher salt, thyme and garlic.

5. Cover the roasting pan with aluminum foil before adding the cover in order to keep as much moisture in as possible and roast in the oven 1½-2 hours.

6. At this point, add the carrots, parsnips, and shallots or pearl onions.

7. Cover and roast for about another hour or until the vegetables are fork tender. Remove the roast and vegetables from the pot and hold in a warm oven, about 200°F, while you prepare the gravy.

8. Skim any excess fat from the top of the stock in the roasting pan, then bring the liquid to a boil on the stove top.

9. Prepare a thickening slurry by shaking or whisking together, until smooth, the flour and warm water in a covered mason jar.

10. Slowly pour the flour slurry into the boiling roasting stock, whisking constantly and quickly so no lumps form in the gravy. Use only as much of the slurry as necessary to bring the gravy to the consistency you like.

Foolproof Dry-Rubbed Oven Ribs

PREP TIME: **20** MINUTES | COOK TIME: **8** HOURS | SERVES **4–6**

I love slow-smoked ribs. It's my favourite way to prepare them during the summer months, but when that's not possible, I make these very simple, dry-rubbed ribs in the oven using my own blend of herbs and spices. This recipe is practically foolproof. Plenty of time but no skill at all is required to produce succulent, fall-apart tender ribs.

These ribs are perfect party food because the spice rub provides all the flavour with no need for messy sauces that always land on your favourite outfit. If you like, however, a favourite glazing barbecue sauce can be brushed on at the end. My kids are quite fond of honey barbecue sauce on these ribs.

4–5 lb of ribs

3 tbsp paprika

2 tbsp smoked paprika

2 tbsp chili powder

3 tbsp kosher salt

1 tbsp powdered ginger

1 tbsp chipotle powder

6 tbsp brown sugar

1 tbsp black pepper

1 tbsp ground nutmeg

1 tbsp ground oregano

1 tbsp ground thyme

1 tbsp ground coriander

2 tbsp dry mustard powder

2 tbsp garlic powder

3 tbsp onion powder

1 tsp ground cumin

1 tsp cinnamon

1. There's a thin membrane called silver skin on the back of all pork ribs that I like to remove first. If left on, it will shrink during cooking and cause the ribs to curl. It also prevents the spice mix from seasoning the underside of the ribs. I push a butter knife between the silver skin and the first bone on the rack of ribs to loosen the skin and create a slit. I then poke my finger into the slit, grasp the silver skin, and pull it off all the way down the length of the rack of ribs.

2. Mix together all the remaining ingredients well and store any unused dry rub in an airtight container in a cool place. Makes about 2 cups dry rub.

3. Liberally rub the spice mix all over the surface of the pork ribs on both sides. Cover with plastic wrap and place in the fridge for several hours or, as I prefer, overnight.

4. Preheat oven to 225°F.

5. Place the ribs, uncovered, on a wire rack over a baking sheet and bake in the oven for 8-9 hours, depending on the thickness of the ribs. Baby-back ribs take less time. Side ribs will likely take the longest. When you pull on one of the bones at the end of the rack and it pulls away easily, they're done. This is the best way to test them.

Honey Barbecue Pulled Beef
Sandwiches *with* Creamy Dijon Coleslaw

PREP TIME: **30** MINUTES | COOK TIME: **3** HOURS | SERVES **6–8**

HONEY BARBECUE PULLED BEEF

3–4 lb blade, chuck, or cross-rib beef roast

salt and pepper to season

2 tbsp vegetable oil

1½ cups plain tomato sauce

1 medium red onion,
very finely diced

4 cloves garlic, finely minced

½–1 tsp chipotle powder
(or to taste)

2 tsp smoked paprika

2 tsp dry mustard powder

½ tsp ground cumin

1 tsp ground thyme

½ tsp ground nutmeg

½ tsp salt

½ tsp black pepper

½ cup honey

¼ cup apple cider vinegar

CREAMY DIJON COLESLAW

2 cups shredded cabbage

1 large grated carrot

½ cup mayonnaise

1½ tbsp whole-grain Dijon mustard

1 tbsp apple cider vinegar

3 tbsp sugar (or 2 tbsp honey)

salt and pepper to season

This is one of our household's go-to recipes whenever we are feeding a large group of people. The recipe can easily be doubled or tripled, as needed, to produce tender beef, slow braised in an easy, smoky homemade barbecue sauce and then served on toasted buns or crusty bread with delicious Creamy Dijon Coleslaw. You can even make it the day before the big game and just pop it into the oven to warm if you have people coming over, or take it along to a potluck if you're the one going out. Make-ahead recipes like this are the perfect way to spend time with your guests rather than fussing in the kitchen.

HONEY BARBECUE PULLED BEEF SANDWICHES

1.   Preheat oven to 325°F.

2.   Season the beef roast with salt and pepper. Heat a couple of tablespoons of vegetable oil in a cast-iron or heavy bottom skillet and then brown the roast on all sides.

3.   Transfer the roast to a covered roasting pan or Dutch oven.

4.   Stir together the tomato sauce, onions, garlic, chipotle powder, smoked paprika, mustard powder, cumin, thyme, nutmeg, salt, and pepper.

5.   Pour over the roast, cover, and cook for about 3 hours, or a little longer for a larger roast, until the meat is tender and falling apart. I like to turn the roast in the sauce halfway through the cooking time.

6.   When cooked, remove the meat, cover with aluminum foil, and transfer the sauce in the pan to a small saucepan.

7.   Add the honey and vinegar to the saucepan and simmer for about 15–20 minutes or until it thickens to a barbecue-sauce consistency.

8. Using a fork (or just your fingers if the roast has cooled down sufficiently) pull the beef apart in small finger-width pieces, removing any excess fat as you go.

9. Pour the hot sauce over the beef.

10. Serve on toasted burger buns or artisan crusty bread. I love to serve it with some Creamy Dijon Coleslaw.

CREAMY DIJON COLESLAW

1. Stir together the mayo, Dijon mustard, vinegar, sugar (or honey), salt, and pepper.

2. Toss together well with the cabbage and carrot.

Easy Lemon Dijon Roasted Chicken

PREP TIME: **10** MINUTES

COOK TIME: **1** HOUR **50** MINUTES (VARIES DEPENDING ON THE SIZE OF THE CHICKEN) | SERVES **4–6**

Here's a super easy and super flavourful way to liven up that Sunday roast-chicken dinner using simple ingredients and a no-fuss method. It's very simple to prepare, and once in the oven, there's practically nothing left to do but wait for the heady aroma to fill the house and get all appetites whetted for a great sit-down family meal. A heated lemon along with more herbs gets added to the chicken cavity to infuse the juicy meat with even more delicious flavour.

one 3–4 lb whole roasting chicken

1 lemon

4 sprigs fresh herbs (cilantro, rosemary, or oregano make good choices, or a combination of your favourites)

4 tbsp Dijon mustard

½ tsp salt

½ tsp black pepper

juice of ½ a lemon

2 tbsp finely minced herbs
I like thyme, sage, and oregano (you can use dried herbs here)

2 cloves garlic, finely minced

1. Preheat oven to 375°F.

2. Clean and pat the chicken dry with paper towels.

3. Using a fork, stab the lemon several times all over its surface. Microwave or boil the lemon for about 30-60 seconds to heat it up and then add it to the cavity of the chicken along with the herbs.

4. In a small bowl, mix together the Dijon mustard, salt, pepper, lemon juice, minced herbs, and minced garlic.

5. Slather the mixture evenly over the entire surface of the chicken. Tuck the wing tips under the chicken and tie the drumsticks together with butcher string.

6. Place on a roasting rack and roast, uncovered, for 20 minutes.

7. Reduce the heat to 350°F and continue to roast for about another 60-90 minutes, depending on the size of your chicken, until the internal temperature of the thickest part of the breast reads 185°F on a meat thermometer. I always use a meat thermometer for roasted meats, including chicken. Not only is it the best way to ensure safe cooking but also, almost as important, to know that you are not overcooking the meat.

8. Do not cover the chicken at all during the cooking time.

9. When fully cooked, remove from the oven and let rest for 10-15 minutes before carving and serving.

Dijon Beef and Mushroom Pie

PREP TIME: **30** MINUTES | COOK TIME: **3** HOURS **30** MINUTES | SERVES **6–8**

DIJON BEEF AND MUSHROOMS

3 lb blade or cross-rib roast, cut in 1-inch cubes

salt and pepper to season

1 cup flour

3 tbsp canola oil

3 cups low-sodium or salt-free beef stock

1 cup button or crimini mushrooms, cut into quarters

3 tbsp butter

4 cloves garlic, chopped

2 shallots, chopped

1 medium red onion, diced

2 large celery stalks, diced

¼ cup Worcestershire sauce

4 tbsp Dijon mustard

1 tsp dried thyme

1 tsp freshly ground nutmeg

½ tsp each of salt and pepper to season

THE PASTRY

½ cup cold salted butter

2 cups all-purpose flour

1 large or extra-large egg, lightly whisked with 1 tbsp water

You can bet for certain that if something's wrapped or topped with pastry, I will eat it, and that sure bet applies as much or more to savoury foods as it does sweets. This amazing recipe is based on a classic English beef and mustard pie, but with a little French twist using Dijon instead. If you have some good English mustard on hand, it will work brilliantly in this recipe as will a great smoked mustard too. We always serve our steamed vegetables and roasted potatoes on the side to complete this incredible comfort-food meal.

DIJON BEEF AND MUSHROOMS

1. Preheat oven to 325°F.

2. Heat a cast-iron skillet over medium-high heat. Season the beef cubes with salt and pepper and dredge them in the flour, coating them on all sides. Discard the unused flour dredge.

3. Add the canola oil to the heated skillet and brown the beef on all sides. Transfer the beef to a 3-quart covered casserole dish. Deglaze the cast-iron skillet with the beef stock and pour over the beef in the casserole dish.

4. In a separate sauté pan, lightly brown the mushrooms in the butter and then add the garlic, shallots, red onion, and celery and cook until the onions have softened. Add to the casserole with the beef and stock. Stir in the Worcestershire sauce, mustard, thyme, nutmeg, and the ½ tsp each of salt and pepper to season.

5. Cover and place in the oven for about 3 hours until the beef is fall-apart tender and the liquid has reduced to a thin gravy.

6. Remove from the oven and skim any excess fat off the surface. You can chill the braised beef overnight and add the pastry the next day, if that's when you're serving it, or let the beef cool for at least 1 hour before adding the pastry topping in advance of serving.

THE PASTRY

1. Preheat oven to 375°F.

2. Using a food processor or a pastry cutter, pulse or cut the butter into the flour until only small pieces of butter are visible in the mix, about the size of small peas.

3. Whisk the egg together with the water and pour over the flour and butter mixture. Mix gently with a wooden spoon until a soft dough forms. Wrap the dough in plastic wrap and chill in the fridge for 30 minutes.

4. Place the dough on a well-floured surface and roll out to approximately 1 inch larger than the length and width of the casserole dish. Cut a small disk the size of a dime out of the center of the dough to let the steam escape.

5. Place the dough on top of the cooled braised beef and mushrooms, pressing it over the edges of the baking dish to get good contact. You can brush an egg wash on top of the pastry if you like to ensure even browning.

6. Bake for about 25-30 minutes or until the top is evenly golden brown and the filling bubbling.

7. Serve immediately with steamed vegetables and, if you like, roasted potatoes.

Spouse is still the Soup Queen at our house. Many of the soup ideas on *RockRecipes.com* are hers, and she often makes the best use of leftover chicken, ham, and other ingredients. She's also the one who reminds me of how frequently people are looking for great side dishes, so this section includes some of our favourites. Spouse says to try the Balsamic and Honey Roasted Beets, you'll love them. I say those Lemon Herb Roasted Potato Nuggets might just beat the beets as a recipe you'll make again and again.

side dishes and soups

Lemon Herb Roasted Potato Nuggets 140

Braised Short-Rib Beef Barley Soup. 142

Ham, Sweet Potato, and Spinach Soup. 144

Chorizo Rotisserie Chicken Noodle Soup 146

Lemon Shrimp Pasta Salad 148

Spinach Pesto Pappardelle 150

Balsamic and Honey Roasted Beets 152

BLT Salad with Creamy Dijon Dressing *and* Garlic Herb Butter Croutons 154

Warm Grilled Potato Salad *with* Lemon and Oregano 156

Newfoundland Figgy Duff 158

Honey Roasted Carrots *with* Mint 160

Warm Roasted Spaghetti Squash and Quinoa Salad 162

Spicy Ginger Orange Noodles 164

Chicken Carrot and Lentil Soup 166

Newfoundland Dressing (Summer Savoury Stuffing) 168

Lemon Herb Roasted Potato Nuggets

PREP TIME: **10** MINUTES | COOK TIME: **1** HOUR | SERVES **4-6**

These beautiful little roasted potato nuggets are famous in their own right at this point, having had hundreds of thousands of views on *RockRecipes.com* as well as hundreds of thousands of shares on social media like Facebook and Pinterest. In fact, this recipe has risen to be the most popular side dish since my blog was established.

Infused with lemon and herb flavour and roasted to crispy perfection, it's no wonder they're so popular. Plus, they go with almost anything from grilled chicken to rack of lamb, making them one of our most versatile side dishes too. Try them and see what all the fuss is about.

6-8 **large-sized russet potatoes**, peeled and cut into 1½- to 2-inch chunks

juice of 1 **lemon**

½ tsp **kosher salt**

½ tsp **cracked black pepper**

1½ tbsp **dried herbs** (oregano, thyme, and rosemary are good choices)

1 **whole garlic bulb**, broken into about 4 pieces (optional)

¼ to ⅓ cup **olive oil** (butter or other oil will work as well; a butter/olive oil combination is very good too)

1. Preheat oven to 375°F.

2. Parboil the potatoes in salted water for about 3-4 minutes, no longer.

3. Meanwhile, heat a baking pan of sufficient size to hold your potatoes without crowding them in the preheated oven. A glass or metal pan is fine, as long as it is well heated beforehand. This will help to prevent the potatoes from sticking to the pan.

4. After parboiling, drain the potatoes and let them stand for 5 minutes. Then toss the potatoes with the lemon juice.

5. Toss together so that the potatoes absorb the lemon juice.

6. Add the salt, pepper, herbs, garlic, and olive oil.

7. Transfer the seasoned potatoes, garlic, and oil to the hot baking pan. These should sizzle as they hit the pan—a good indication they will not stick. Roast the potatoes for about 60-75 minutes or until they are nicely golden brown all over, turning them every 20 minutes or so. After the first 10 minutes, give the pan a shake to make sure the potatoes are not stuck. The roasted garlic may have to be removed before the potatoes are finished as it generally cooks faster.

Braised Short-Rib Beef Barley Soup

PREP TIME: **30** MINUTES | COOK TIME: **3** HOURS | SERVES **6**

Beef short ribs have some of the deepest, richest flavour of any cut of meat. The slow braising here not only brings out their intense beefy flavour, but helps to provide added richness to the broth as well in this very hearty and satisfying soup. This is the kind of soup ideally suited as a slow-cooked winter weekend meal, perhaps with some freshly baked bread or rolls to enjoy with it.

2½ lb **beef short ribs**

salt and **pepper** to season

½ cup **flour** for dredging (approx.)

3–4 tbsp **vegetable oil**

2 **large red onions**, diced small

4 **cloves garlic**, minced

6 cups of **low-sodium** or **no-salt-added beef stock**

4 cups **canned tomato puree**

½ tsp **black pepper**

½ tsp **kosher salt**

2 tsp **dried thyme**

1 tbsp **brown sugar**

1 tsp **freshly ground nutmeg**

1 rounded tsp **smoked paprika**

⅓ cup **pearl barley**

4 **large carrots**, diced small

1. Preheat oven to 300°F.

2. Season the short ribs with salt and pepper and dredge them in the flour, covering them in an even coat on all sides. Throw out any excess flour.

3. Heat the vegetable oil in a cast-iron skillet over medium to medium-high heat and brown the short ribs on both sides.

4. Transfer the browned ribs to a covered roasting pan or Dutch oven.

5. Add the onions, garlic, and 2 cups of the beef stock.

6. Slow cook for at least a couple of hours until the meat is tender and falling off the bones.

7. Remove the ribs from the pot, skim off any excess fat from the braising liquid, and pour it into a 6- to 8-quart pot.

8. Add the remaining 4 cups beef stock along with the pureed tomatoes, pepper, salt, thyme, sugar, nutmeg, and smoked paprika. Simmer for about 20 minutes.

9. While the soup is simmering, remove all of the meat from the short ribs by pulling it off in small pieces with a fork. Remove any excess fat, leaving only the tender meat behind.

10. After 20 minutes, add the beef to the soup pot along with the barley and carrots.

11. Simmer for another 20 minutes or so until the carrots and barley are cooked.

12. In the last 10 minutes of cooking time, taste the broth to determine if it needs any additional seasoning.

13. I prefer this soup a little on the thick side, but if you prefer a thinner soup, you can easily add another couple of cups of beef stock at any stage after the beef has cooked.

Ham, Sweet Potato, and Spinach Soup

PREP TIME: **15** MINUTES | COOK TIME: **30** MINUTES | SERVES **4–6**

Although good old Newfoundland Pea Soup is still the most common use of leftover baked ham at our house, sometimes a quick soup is a much-appreciated Leftover Rescue Recipe when time is at a premium. This is a beautifully colourful, flavourful, and nutritious soup that really fits the bill.

This versatile recipe is also great as a vegetarian soup if you eliminate the ham, or just remove a serving or two for your vegetarian guests before adding the ham at the end. Substitute leftover chicken and chicken stock for another delicious version too.

2 tbsp **olive oil**

4 **cloves garlic**, minced

3 **large shallots**, diced

6 cups **salt-free** or **low-sodium vegetable stock**

2 **bay leaves**

6 **sprigs fresh thyme** (or 2 tsp whole dry thyme leaves)

2 tsp **yellow curry powder** (optional)

1 tsp **freshly ground black pepper**

1 tsp **freshly grated nutmeg**

1½–2 cups diced **sweet potato**

½ cup **dry red lentils**

1 cup diced **sweet bell peppers**

2½–3 cups **leftover diced baked ham**

1 cup chopped **baby spinach leaves**

1. Add the olive oil, garlic, and shallots to a 3- or 4-quart pot or Dutch oven over medium heat.

2. Sauté only until the shallots soften then add the vegetable stock, bay leaves, thyme, curry powder, pepper, and nutmeg.

3. Bring to a simmer and add the sweet potato and lentils.

4. Simmer over low heat until the sweet potatoes are almost fork tender and the lentils cooked.

5. Add the bell peppers and ham. Simmer for only about 5-6 minutes.

6. Remove from heat and ladle into serving bowls along with ¼ cup chopped baby spinach per bowl. Pour the broth over the spinach to wilt it while preserving its colour, making for a more appealing presentation.

tip > I sometimes roast the diced sweet potato after tossing it in a little olive oil and seasoning with salt and pepper. This adds a little roasted flavour and helps keep the sweet potato from falling apart. When doing this, I add the sweet potatoes at the end with the peppers.

Chorizo Rotisserie Chicken Noodle Soup

PREP TIME: **1** HOUR | COOK TIME: **30** MINUTES | SERVES **6**

SOUP STOCK

bones from 1 **cooked supermarket rotisserie chicken**

8–10 cups **water**

1 **onion**, cut in quarters

1 **carrot**, roughly chopped

3 **cloves garlic**, crushed

CHORIZO ROTISSERIE CHICKEN NOODLE SOUP

chicken stock prepared earlier

2 tbsp **summer savoury**

3 **carrots**, cut in coins or sticks

1 cup **medium egg noodles**, uncooked

1 **red bell pepper**, diced

meat from the rotisserie chicken, cubed

6 oz chopped **chorizo sausage**

salt and **pepper** to season

You can pick up a rotisserie chicken in practically any super-market these days for a quick family dinner that doesn't come in a bucket, which in my book is a good thing. When I do buy a cooked chicken like this, I still like to make the most of the leftovers so nothing goes to waste. This terrific recipe shows how to make a simple stock to stretch that leftover chicken into a second delicious meal. The addition of a little chorizo sausage brings a smoky note to the broth for a tasty twist on a comfort-food favourite soup.

SOUP STOCK

1. Remove most of the meat from a rotisserie chicken, cut it in large cubes and set aside for later.

2. Slowly simmer the chicken bones in the water along with the onion, carrot, and garlic. Simmer gently for about an hour. Strain the stock through a cheesecloth-lined colander. Skim off any excess fat that comes to the surface. You can make the stock a day ahead if you like and refrigerate it overnight, which makes the fat that comes to the surface much easier to remove.

CHORIZO ROTISSERIE CHICKEN NOODLE SOUP

1. Add the prepared chicken stock, savoury, and carrots to a large soup pot. Simmer for about 15 minutes before adding the egg noodles, red pepper, cubed cooked chicken breasts, and chorizo sausage.

2. Season with salt and pepper as needed. Simmer until the noodles are tender and serve.

Lemon Shrimp Pasta Salad

PREP TIME: **15** MINUTES | COOK TIME: **15** MINUTES | SERVES **4–6**

SHRIMP PASTA

2½ cups **cooked pasta**, rinsed and cooled

1½ cups **small cooked shrimp**, peeled and de-veined

½ cup thinly sliced **red bell pepper**

½ cup julienne **fresh snow peas**

LOW-FAT LEMON DRESSING

⅔ cup **plain Greek yogurt**

zest of 1 **lemon**, finely grated

juice of 1 **lemon**

2 **cloves garlic**, finely minced

4 tbsp **olive oil**

1½ tbsp **honey**

salt and **pepper** to season

2 tbsp chopped **chives**

This super easy lemon shrimp pasta salad uses an easy to prepare, low-fat, yogurt-based dressing for a tangy complement to the substantial bites of pasta. Some julienne slivers of fresh, sweet snow peas add colour, flavour, and great crunch too. It makes a sensibly delicious addition to a summer BBQ table or as a side dish or tasty lunch at any time of the year.

SHRIMP PASTA

1. Cook the pasta to al dente and rinse well with cold water.

2. Leave the pasta to drain well while you prepare the dressing and the rest of the salad.

3. The pasta, shrimp, bell pepper, and snow peas will be added when the dressing is ready.

LOW-FAT LEMON DRESSING

1. Whisk together all of the ingredients and let it sit for 20 minutes if time allows. This allows the lemon zest to infuse flavour into the dressing.

2. If you like a thinner dressing, you can always add a little more lemon juice or even a little skim milk.

3. Toss together the dressing with the shrimp, pasta, peppers, and snow peas.

tip > Explore the many different shapes and sizes available in the pasta aisle to make your pasta salads and other pasta dishes more interesting. The pasta shown here is called *dischi volante*, which translates as "flying saucers." What kid wouldn't want to eat flying saucers for dinner?

Spinach Pesto Pappardelle

PREP TIME: 20 MINUTES | **COOK TIME: 10 MINUTES** | **SERVES 4**

4 cups (approx.) **baby spinach leaves** (or 1 cup wilted spinach)

½ cup **grated Parmesan cheese**

pinch **black pepper**

¼ cup **toasted pine nuts**

2 **cloves garlic**, finely minced

½ cup good quality **extra-virgin olive oil**

This recipe is a delicious way to bring some nutritious spinach to the plate without complaints. My kids even eat the cold leftovers as a pasta salad the next day.

Blanching the spinach assures it will keep its bright green colour in the pesto, which can be kept in the fridge for a couple of days. Use less oil for a thicker pesto that can be served as a party dip with thin slices of crusty bread. I also love serving small bowls of pasta like this as an appetizer course at a celebration dinner, but it's also a terrific simple side dish to serve with grilled fish or chicken.

1. Have a large bowl of ice water standing by. Drop the spinach into boiling water for only about 30 seconds.

2. Drain immediately and plunge the spinach into the ice water.

3. Drain and lay the spinach out on a few layers of paper towels and pat them dry before adding them to a blender or food processor along with the Parmesan, pepper, pine nuts, and garlic.

4. I toast the pine nuts in the oven on a cookie sheet for a few minutes, but you can toss them in a non-stick sauté pan for a couple of minutes until they begin to brown a little. Either way, watch them carefully—they can burn quickly.

5. Process on medium speed until the spinach and other ingredients begin to form a paste, then reduce the speed to low and begin slowly drizzling in the olive oil. If you want to use the pesto as a dip, you can cut back on the amount of olive oil to make it thicker.

6. Makes enough pesto to coat about ½ lb dry pasta, like pappardelle, when cooked.

7. Store any leftovers in the fridge in an airtight container.

Balsamic and Honey Roasted Beets

PREP TIME: **10** MINUTES | COOK TIME: **1** HOUR | SERVES **6–8**

This beautiful side dish comes courtesy of Spouse, who was the first to make them at our house. Beets are only second to parsnip as her favourite root vegetable, and roasting them is her preferred method to bring out all of their intense flavour. Roasted beets are delicious just tossed with salt, pepper, and a drizzle of olive oil, but the addition of another couple of simple ingredients like honey and balsamic vinegar adds a beautiful, glistening, and very tasty glaze you'll love.

> tip > These warm roasted beets also make a phenomenal addition to any salad, but adding them to spinach and goat cheese salad is a particular favourite of mine. I also like to add toasted walnuts and toss the whole works in a simple balsamic vinaigrette for an outstanding starter course at dinner or as a tasty lunch.

2 lb **fresh beets**, peeled and cubed

½ tsp **salt**

½ tsp **black pepper**

2 tbsp **olive oil**

3 tbsp **balsamic vinegar**

2 tbsp **honey**

1 tsp chopped **fresh thyme** (optional)

1. Preheat oven to 350°F.

2. Peel the beets and cut them into roughly 1- to 1½-inch cubes.

3. Toss the beets in the salt, pepper, and olive oil.

4. Roast in a single layer for about 45 minutes, tossing occasionally.

5. Toss the partially roasted beets in the honey and balsamic vinegar and add the thyme too if you are using it.

6. Return to the oven and roast for an additional 15 minutes or so, tossing occasionally until the beets are fork tender.

BLT Salad *with* Creamy Dijon Dressing and Garlic Herb Butter Croutons

PREP TIME: 20 MINUTES | **COOK TIME: 10 MINUTES** | **SERVES 4**

BLT SALAD

1 small head **romaine lettuce**, washed, dried, and chopped

2 **tomatoes**, cut in wedges

6 **radishes**, sliced (optional)

½ lb **crisp-cooked bacon**

GARLIC AND HERB BUTTER CROUTONS

6 slices **day-old bread**, cubed

2 **cloves garlic**, minced

2 tbsp chopped **fresh herbs** (thyme and oregano work well)

¼ cup **melted butter**

CREAMY DIJON DRESSING

½ cup **mayonnaise**

2 tbsp **Dijon mustard**

3 tbsp **honey**

2 tbsp **apple cider vinegar**

pinch **salt** and **pepper**

This BLT salad recipe is a result of laziness. The first time I made it, we were short of salad fixings in the fridge, and I just didn't want to go shopping, so what went in the salad was just what was on hand.

As compensation for lack of ingredients, I just added *a lot* of bacon! Besides the bacon, the homemade garlic and herb butter croutons give amazing flavour and crunch to this salad, and the creamy Dijon dressing is just the perfect finishing touch. It may not be the most complex of salads, but it's turned out to be a family favourite and is always in high demand when we have friends over for backyard barbecues in the summer.

BLT SALAD

1. Assemble all of the salad ingredients onto 4 individual serving plates.

GARLIC AND HERB BUTTER CROUTONS

1. Preheat oven to 350°F.

2. Place the bread cubes on a baking sheet and bake for 10-15 minutes or until the cubes are golden brown and crispy. Toss them a couple of times during the baking time.

3. Combine the garlic and melted butter in a small saucepan and cook over low heat for just a few minutes until the garlic softens, then add the chopped herbs. Pour over the baked croutons and toss well.

4. Divide the croutons evenly over the prepared salad plates.

CREAMY DIJON DRESSING

1. Add all of the ingredients in the dressing to a small glass bowl and whisk together well.

2. If you can, let the dressing sit in the fridge for an hour or so before serving.

3. Drizzle the dressing all over the salad and croutons just before serving.

Warm Grilled Potato Salad
with Lemon and Oregano

PREP TIME: **15** MINUTES | COOK TIME: **15** MINUTES | SERVES **4–6**

As regular readers of *RockRecipes.com* will know, our family practically lives off the backyard grill in the summer months. With the season so short here in Newfoundland, nobody blames us for taking as much advantage of the grilling season as we possibly can. Simple grilled fish, chops, steaks, and chicken get regular rotation in our meal planning, but like so many other folks, the real challenge with summer grilling is the question, "What are we going to serve with it?"

This recipe answers the question with a side dish that comes off the grill as well and includes plenty of bright, fresh summertime flavours.

12 **medium-sized red potatoes,** sliced

a few tsp **olive oil** for brushing on the potatoes

salt and **pepper** to season

2–3 tbsp **extra-virgin olive oil**

½ **small red bell pepper,** finely diced

zest of 1 **lemon,** finely grated

juice of 1 **lemon**

2 tbsp chopped **fresh oregano**

2 tbsp chopped **fresh chives**

2–3 oz **feta cheese**

1. Cut the potatoes into ½-inch slices and gently parboil them in lightly salted water for 4 or 5 minutes or until a fork can be pushed through a slice while it's still not soft or fully cooked.

2. Drain the potatoes and let them cool on a clean tea towel in a single layer. When they are cool enough to handle, transfer them to a cookie sheet and very lightly brush each side of the potatoes with the olive oil and lightly season with salt and pepper.

3. Take them off the cookie sheet and grill on medium heat until they are golden brown, fully cooked, and fork tender. Remove from the grill and place in a large heatproof bowl.

4. Whisk together the 2-3 tbsp extra-virgin olive oil, diced red pepper, lemon juice and zest, oregano, and chives. Pour over the grilled potatoes and toss gently until the potatoes are fully coated.

5. Transfer the potatoes to a serving platter and crumble feta cheese over the top, if desired, when serving.

Newfoundland Figgy Duff

PREP TIME: 10 MINUTES | COOK TIME: 1 HOUR 30 MINUTES | SERVES 8

I'm hesitant to even call this Figgy Duff because no definitive recipe for this classic Newfoundland side dish really exists. This one might be more rightly called Port-de-Grave Duff because that's where my grandmother, Belinda Morgan, was from, and this recipe is as close to what I could glean from watching her throw a bit of this and a bit of that into her mixing bowl practically every Sunday morning of her life. Regional versions and individual family versions abound, some including breadcrumbs, spices, or molasses, for example. But this is the Figgy Duff we know in my extended family.

You will notice from the recipe that Figgy Duff has nothing to do with figs. Raisins have been commonly referred to as figs in Newfoundland for many years as I am told is true of the Cornish coast in England, where the historical connection may well lie. It may take mainlanders reading this recipe a while to wrap their heads around a side dish that can also be a dessert. But we islanders are an adaptable bunch. It is indeed traditionally served on the plate with a roast dinner or Jiggs Dinner, but it can also be served as a dessert with a rum-and-butter or brown-sugar sauce.

2 cups **flour**

½ cup **sugar**

2 tsp **baking powder**

1 cup **raisins**

⅓ cup **melted butter**

¾ cup **milk**

2 tsp **vanilla extract**

1. Sift together the flour, sugar, and baking powder.

2. Add the raisins and toss well.

3. Add the melted butter, milk, and vanilla.

4. Mix all together with a wooden spoon just until a soft dough is formed. Put dough into a pudding steamer or a wet, heavy cotton pudding bag, tying the bag with a piece of butcher string but leaving about an inch of slack at the top to allow the pudding to expand. Boil for approximately 1½ hours. This is most often done in the pot with the boiled root vegetables, cabbage, and salt beef included in a Jiggs Dinner, but can be done in a pot on its own as well.

note > You can substitute the sugar for ½ cup molasses and adjust the milk accordingly to form the proper consistency of the dough. Spices like 1 tsp cinnamon and ½ tsp allspice can also be added as variations. One of my favourite ways to enjoy the leftovers of this steamed pudding is to fry leftover slices in butter and serve with a drizzle of molasses.

Honey Roasted Carrots *with* Mint

PREP TIME: **10** MINUTES | COOK TIME: **30** MINUTES | SERVES **4–6**

This is one of the most common side dishes you will find throughout the year on my Sunday dinner table. Whatever roast dinner is on the menu—be it prime rib, turkey, lamb, ham, or chicken—you're likely to find these carrots served beside it. Since we so often have roasted potatoes with our Sunday dinners, it makes sense to roast the other vegetables too as we do with parsnip and beets as well. I'm not suggesting you abandon your much-loved boiled veggies altogether, but roasting does bring out their natural sweetness and makes for a nice change from time to time.

8 **medium carrots**, peeled and cut into sticks or slices

¼ tsp **white pepper**

2 tbsp **honey**

3 tbsp **olive oil**

2 tbsp chopped **fresh mint**

1. Preheat oven to 375°F.

2. Toss all ingredients together, except the mint, and turn onto a parchment-lined baking pan in a single layer.

3. Bake for about 15 minutes.

4. After 15 minutes, toss carrots in pan and add the chopped mint.

5. Roast for about another 15 minutes or until the carrots are fork tender.

6. Serve immediately.

Warm Roasted Spaghetti Squash
and Quinoa Salad

PREP TIME: **15** MINUTES | COOK TIME: **45** MINUTES | SERVES **4**

This salad is an invention of Spouse's created to make use of some already cooked quinoa in the fridge. She added ginger for warmth and lemon for brightness to the quickly stir-fried peppers and onions and served it over sweet roasted spaghetti squash. This makes a terrific healthy side dish, but I'd even serve it as a vegetarian lunch or with lean grilled chicken, pork, or fish.

ROASTED SQUASH

1 **large spaghetti squash**

salt and **pepper** to season

1 tbsp **olive oil**

QUINOA SALAD

½ cup **quinoa**

2 cups **water** (or chicken stock)

½ tsp **salt**

2 tbsp **olive oil**

2 **cloves garlic**, minced

1 **small red onion**, diced

1 cup chopped **red bell pepper**

1 tbsp **finely grated ginger**

½ tsp **Chinese five-spice powder**

zest and juice of 1 **lemon**

salt and **pepper** to season

ROASTED SQUASH

1. Preheat oven to 375°F.

2. Cut the squash in half and remove the seeds and fibers from the center. Season with salt and pepper and brush the inside surfaces with the olive oil.

3. Place on a baking sheet and roast for about 40 minutes or until fork tender. Use a fork to scrape out the cooked "spaghetti" strings of squash.

QUINOA SALAD

1. Slowly simmer the quinoa in the salted water (or chicken stock) for about 20 minutes until fully cooked. Quinoa should be cooked in a similar way as rice. I always turn the heat off for the last 5 minutes, cover, and let sit, then fluff with a fork at the end.

2. Heat the 2 tbsp oil over medium heat and add the garlic and red onion until they begin to soften.

3. Quickly add the peppers and stir-fry for 1 minute before adding the ginger, five-spice powder, lemon zest and juice, and salt and pepper.

4. Stir-fry for only a few minutes before serving over the roasted spaghetti squash.

5. Top with green onions and a drizzle of extra-virgin olive oil if you like.

Spicy Ginger Orange Noodles

PREP TIME: **15** MINUTES | COOK TIME: **15** MINUTES | SERVES **4–6**

Here's a versatile, quick and easy side dish that we serve with many main dishes at our house, especially Asian inspired recipes like the Glazed Sesame Chicken (page 16). Just substituting the orange juice and zest easily makes a lemon version too. As the recipe notes, practically any vegetables you have on hand can be substituted to create a slightly different but equally delicious side dish every time.

one 10–12 oz package **thin egg noodles** or **rice noodles**

3 tbsp **extra-virgin olive oil**

3 tbsp **butter**

1 cup julienne cut **carrots**

4 **cloves garlic**, minced

½ tsp **black pepper**

pinch **salt**

3 tbsp **grated fresh ginger root**

juice of 1 **large orange**

zest of 1 **large orange**, finely grated or minced

1 tsp **crushed chili paste** or a pinch of chili flakes (more or less to taste)

½ cup **canned bamboo shoots**, rinsed (or water chestnuts)

1. Cook the noodles in salted water. Drain but do not rinse.

2. In a large wok or sauté pan over medium heat, add the olive oil and butter. Add the julienne cut carrots and sauté for a couple of minutes before adding the garlic.

3. Cook for only a minute or so to soften but not brown the garlic.

4. Add the pepper, salt, ginger, orange juice and zest, and chili paste.

5. As soon as this starts to simmer, add the bamboo shoots or water chestnuts.

6. Toss together for a minute or so to warm the vegetables through.

7. The noodles should be added at this point, immediately after they are drained while still piping hot. This makes them easier to coat evenly.

8. Toss together very well over the heat for a few minutes and serve immediately with the green onions or fresh chives sprinkled on top.

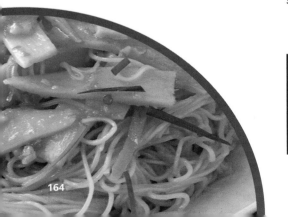

note > This is a versatile base recipe in which you can substitute many other vegetables of your choice like bell peppers, bok choi, scallions, broccoli, snow peas, etcetera. At our house we generally use whatever is on hand.

Chicken Carrot and Lentil Soup

PREP TIME: **10** MINUTES | COOK TIME: **35** MINUTES | SERVES **6–8**

One of the quickest, easiest and most wholesome soups I know, this recipe makes great use of leftover roast chicken. For the most part, it is just an "add everything to the pot" kind of soup that's practically foolproof. Try it with leftover turkey too for an equally delicious soup after the holidays.

2 tbsp **olive oil**

1 **medium red onion**, chopped

3 **cloves garlic**, minced

3 **bay leaves**

6–8 cups **low-sodium** or **salt-free chicken stock**

1 cup of **yellow lentils**

1½ cups of diced **carrots**

1½ cups diced **celery**

2 tbsp chopped **fresh thyme**

salt and **pepper** to season

2–3 cups diced cooked **chicken**

1. Heat olive oil in a Dutch oven or large saucepan over medium heat. Add the onions and garlic and cook for just a few minutes until the onions soften but do not brown.

2. Add all of the remaining ingredients at once, *except* the chicken and simmer for about 30 minutes until the lentils have cooked and broken down and the carrots are fully cooked.

3. Add the chicken to the pot in the last 5 minutes or so of cooking time to thoroughly reheat it before serving.

note > You can vary the thickness of this soup by controlling the amount of stock you use. The soup pictured used only 6 cups of stock to give it a creamier, more pea soup-like consistency. Use more stock and cook for a shorter time, just until the carrots are fork tender, for a more broth-based soup.

Newfoundland Dressing (Summer Savoury Stuffing)

PREP TIME: **10** MINUTES | COOK TIME: **30** MINUTES | SERVES **4**

I'd hazard to say that this stuffing, or as it's known locally, "dressing," has been made in practically every kitchen in the province. For decades, it has been the traditional stuffing for poultry, game birds and even as I've sometimes seen, baked squid. Summer savoury is an annual plant with a sweet mild flavour; not to be confused with winter savoury, which has a much stronger more pungent flavour. They are not interchangeable.

I add garlic and chicken stock to my dressing nowadays for extra flavour and moisture but when I was growing up we would have only used bread crumbs, savoury, melted butter and onions. I most often do not stuff poultry these days, preferring to make any stuffing separately, so the added stock replicates juices that would have ben absorbed in the cavity of the bird.

½ **small onion**, chopped

1 **clove garlic**, minced (optional)

4 tbsp **melted butter**

4 cups **coarse breadcrumbs**

4 tbsp **dried savoury** (i.e., summer savoury)

salt and **pepper** to season

½ cup **chicken stock**

1. In a small skillet, slowly sauté the chopped onion (and garlic if desired) in the butter over low heat until the onions are soft. Meanwhile combine the breadcrumbs, savoury, salt and pepper in a large bowl. Add the cooked onions and chicken stock and toss well to combine all the ingredients.

2. Use as a stuffing for any poultry, including game birds.

3. To cook in the oven, just place in a small covered casserole dish and bake in a low oven 250-300°F for about 30 minutes. You may want to add a little more stock when using this method.

tip > When using this dressing to make stuffed chicken breasts as pictured, add a beaten egg to the stock before adding it to the other ingredients. The egg acts as a binder which keeps the dressing together and allows the stuffed boneless breasts to be easily sliced for a neater presentation when plating.

After publishing the first *Rock Recipes* cookbook, I was delighted to find that people loved the fact that there was a section dedicated to brunch. It seems that I'm not the only one who has grown to love the idea of casual entertaining with a delicious weekend mid-morning meal. Fresh-baked coffee cakes, muffins, scones, or rolls are almost always the star of our family's weekly brunches, and many of the most popular dishes from *RockRecipes.com* have made their way into this book. Thanks to these tasty recipes, treating family and friends to a delicious brunch will always be worth a little bit of an earlier rise on at least one weekend day.

brunch

Newfoundland Raisin Tea Buns 172

Blueberry Buckle. 174

Sunken Grape Almond Cake 176

Cherry Muffins *with* Graham Crumb Streusel 178

Strawberry Muffles 180

Perfect Hot Cross Buns 182

Blueberry Lemon Cornmeal Pancakes. 184

Oatmeal Apple Banana Muffins 186

Sour Cream Lemon Scones 188

Apple Cinnamon Sticky Buns 190

Sausage and Garlic Quiche *with* Smoked Cheddar Sauce 192

Garlic Parmesan Potato Latkes 194

Raspberry Filled Donut Muffins. 196

Newfoundland Raisin Tea Buns

PREP TIME: **15** MINUTES | COOK TIME: **25** MINUTES | MAKES **16–18** LARGE TEA BUNS

3 cups flour

¾ cup sugar

4 tsp baking powder

½ tsp salt

¾ cup butter

1–1½ cups raisins (light or dark, your preference)

2 tbsp lemon juice

2 tsp vanilla extract

1 cup undiluted evaporated milk

This is another iconic recipe in traditional Newfoundland cuisine. It would be nearly impossible to find a single person raised in this province whose mother or grandmother did not bake this incredibly popular Newfoundland baking staple. Again, you will get plenty of variations in family recipes, but this version is one I've made for many years based upon the way my Grandmother Morgan made them during my childhood. Many expatriate Newfoundlanders have discovered *Rock Recipes* by searching for this recipe online. I would not be able to count the rave reviews or the expressions of gratitude for posting this recipe that I have received from all over the world.

1. Preheat oven to 375°F.

2. I start these in my food processor because it's so fast, but they can be made just as easily in a large bowl by cutting the butter in with a pastry blender or just rubbing it into the dry ingredients using your hands like Nan did.

3. In a food processor, combine the flour, sugar, baking powder, and salt.

4. Pulse in the butter until the mixture resembles a coarse meal with small pieces of butter still visible.

5. Add the raisins and make a well in the center of the mixture.

6. Mix together the lemon juice, vanilla extract, and undiluted evaporated milk.

7. Pour the liquid mixture into the well and mix only enough to form a dough ball.

8. Roll on a floured surface to 1 inch thickness and cut out buns with a biscuit cutter and place on parchment-lined baking sheet.

9. Bake for 20-25 minutes or until golden brown. But remember that baking time will vary depending on the size of your biscuit cutter.

Blueberry Buckle

PREP TIME: **20** MINUTES | COOK TIME: **40** MINUTES | SERVES **12**

BLUEBERRY CAKE BASE

½ cup butter

¾ cup sugar

2 eggs

2 tsp vanilla extract

2 cups flour

2 tsp baking powder

1 cup milk

2½ cups fresh blueberries

STREUSEL CRUMB TOPPING

½ cup all-purpose flour

½ cup brown sugar

¼ tsp cinnamon

¼ cup cold butter, cut in small cubes

I first heard of blueberry buckle in a restaurant in Maine many years ago while on vacation. Acting like a typical tourist, I asked where the name originated, but the server seemed to have no idea. "That's what we've always called it" was her only response. It's hard to fault her lack of knowledge on the origin of the name, especially when references to "buckle" as a dessert dish can be dated back to colonial times in the US. With that long a history, it certainly qualifies as a well-loved, old-fashioned comfort food. A little research does indicate that the name comes from the crinkled or "buckled" appearance of the streusel crumb topping as the cake batter rises.

BLUEBERRY CAKE BASE

1. Grease a 10-inch springform pan well and line the bottom with parchment paper, if you like, for easy release of the cake when it is baked.

2. Cream together the butter and sugar until light and fluffy.

3. Add the eggs, one at a time. Beat well after the addition of each egg.

4. Beat in the vanilla extract.

5. Sift together the flour and baking powder.

6. Add dry ingredients alternately with the milk. Always begin and end with an addition of dry ingredients. As a general rule, add the flour mixture in 3 divisions and the milk in 2.

note > I developed this Blueberry Buckle recipe on my own, and I've since used it with other berries and chopped fruit in season and even used frozen berries on occasion, so it really is a versatile year-round recipe.

7.   Be careful not to overmix the batter, or your cake will be dense. Fold the batter only until the flour is incorporated but no more.

8.   Quickly fold in the blueberries.

9.   Spread batter evenly into the prepared pan.

STREUSEL CRUMB TOPPING

1.   Preheat oven to 350°F.

2.   Mix together the flour, sugar, and cinnamon.

3.   Using your fingertips, rub the butter through the dry mixture until it resembles a coarse meal.

4.   Press the crumb mixture together in handfuls and break off small pieces about the size of the top of your pinky finger, scattering them over the surface of the batter already in the pan.

5.   Bake for about 35-40 minutes or until a toothpick inserted in the center comes out clean. The baking time can vary, especially if you use frozen berries. In that case, it may take 10-15 minutes more to bake. The toothpick test is the best way to ensure that this cake is fully baked.

Sunken Grape Almond Cake

PREP TIME: **20** MINUTES | COOK TIME: **1** HOUR | SERVES **12**

I first saw this brunch idea on an Italian cooking show some years ago where they made a grape cake to celebrate the beginning of harvest. It came to mind late last summer when I saw some sweet and tart little Coronation grapes from southern Ontario, which were in season at the time. They are related to Concord grapes, which, like any small grape variety, could be easily substituted.

This buttery, nutty almond cake with little pops of sweet tart flavour needs only a light dusting of icing sugar to complete it, but a dollop of freshly whipped cream when serving would be an excellent addition too.

1 cup toasted ground almonds

1¼ cups sifted all-purpose flour

½ tsp baking powder

pinch salt

1 cup butter

1⅓ cups sugar

1 tsp vanilla extract

1 tsp almond extract

3 eggs

1 tsp lemon zest, finely minced

2 cups small grapes

1. Grease a 10-inch springform pan and line the bottom with parchment paper for easy release of the cake after it's baked. Preheat oven to 325°F.

2. Sift together the ground almonds, flour, baking powder, and salt and set aside.

3. Cream together the butter, sugar, vanilla extract, and almond extract until light and fluffy.

4. Beat in the eggs one at a time, then stir in the lemon zest.

5. Mix in the dry ingredients until the batter is smooth, and spread it evenly into the prepared pan.

6. Place small grapes all over the surface of the batter about a ¼ inch apart. Any variety of small grape will work, or you can use small pitted cherries or large blueberries instead. Do not push them into the batter. Just drop them onto the surface.

7. Bake for about 50-60 minutes or until evenly brown on top and a wooden toothpick inserted in the center comes out clean. Cool in the pan for 20 minutes before releasing the cake to cool on a wire rack. If you are serving the cake warm, you should still wait the 20 minutes to allow it to settle before cutting.

tip > I toast whole almonds in a preheated 350°F oven for 5-8 minutes on a cookie sheet, tossing them at least once. I then grind them very finely in a food processor. Be sure to lightly pack the ground almonds into the measuring cup.

Cherry Muffins *with* Graham Crumb Streusel

PREP TIME: **20** MINUTES | COOK TIME: **30** MINUTES | MAKES **12**

These are beautifully and lightly flavoured muffins with ripe cherries at the center and a topping of crispy, buttery graham cracker crumb streusel. They are delicious, impressive, and probably much easier than you think to prepare.

The recipe came about one Sunday when I was trying to decide whether to make a cherry cheesecake for dessert that night or to use the cherries in a new muffin recipe for brunch. The muffins won out, but thinking about the two options, I decided to incorporate an idea from what would have been a graham crumb base for the cheesecake into a streusel topping for the muffins. Needless to say, they were a huge hit and have been repeatedly requested by brunch guests ever since.

CHERRY MUFFINS

2 cups flour

2 tsp baking powder

1 cup sugar

2 large eggs

⅓ cup canola oil

1 tsp vanilla extract

¼ tsp almond extract (optional)

¾ cup milk

24 fresh pitted cherries

GRAHAM CRUMB STREUSEL

⅓ cup graham cracker crumbs

⅓ cup flour

3 tbsp brown sugar

¼ cup butter

CHERRY MUFFINS

1. Grease a 12-muffin pan very well, including the top of the pan in case the batter blooms over the edges.

2. Sift together the flour and baking powder and set aside.

3. Whisk together the sugar, eggs, canola oil, and extract(s).

4. Stir in the milk.

5. Add the dry ingredients all at once, and stir only until the flour is incorporated. Don't overmix or your muffins risk becoming too dense. Some small lumps in the batter are perfectly fine.

6. Fill the muffin pans half-full with batter.

7. Lay 2 cherries on top of the batter and spoon the remaining batter over the cherries.

8. Top with the Graham Crumb Streusel.

GRAHAM CRUMB STREUSEL

1. Preheat the oven to 350°F.

2. Rub all of the ingredients together with your hands until the butter is fully incorporated into the dry ingredients and the mixture holds together when pressed together in fistfuls.

3. Press the streusel together in small handfuls and break off small pieces about the size of the top of your little finger. Sprinkle them over the muffin batter in the pans.

4. Bake for 25-30 minutes or until the centers of the muffins spring back to the touch and a wooden toothpick inserted into the center turns out clean.

5. Cool on a wire rack for about 15 minutes before attempting to remove them from the pan.

Strawberry Muffles

½ cup butter

¾ cup sugar

2 eggs

3 tsp vanilla extract

2 cups flour

2 tsp baking powder

1 cup milk

1½ cups sliced fresh strawberries

What are strawberry muffles? A muffle is a waffle made from muffin batter, of course. Once, when I was baking up a batch of strawberry muffins for brunch, as an experiment, I took half the muffin batter and made these delicious waffles from it. It was a very successful and tasty experiment indeed. Maybe I got lucky with this particular muffin batter, but the waffles were crispy with a soft, tender center and plenty of juicy strawberry chunks. This strawberry version is delicious, but it will work with other berries or chopped stone fruits like peaches or nectarines as well.

1. Cream together the butter and sugar until fluffy.

2. Add the eggs, one at a time, and vanilla extract. Beat well after each addition of egg.

3. Sift together the flour and baking powder.

4. Add dry ingredients alternately with the milk. Always begin and end with an addition of dry ingredients. As a general rule, add the flour mixture in 3 divisions and the milk in two.

5. To ensure each muffle gets an even distribution of strawberries, I add them to each individual one while cooking. The 1½ cup measurement is approximate. You may use less if you prefer.

6. Heat your waffle iron.

7. My waffle iron takes about ⅓ cup batter per waffle. I spread half of that amount in the waffle iron, sprinkle on several of the strawberry chunks, then top with the second half of the batter before closing the lid and fully cooking the waffle for about 4-5 minutes until golden brown.

8. Serve with maple syrup.

Perfect Hot Cross Buns

PREP TIME: **30** MINUTES + **90** MINUTES RISING TIME | COOK TIME: **35** MINUTES | MAKES **12**

HOT CROSS BUNS

¾ cup lukewarm water (around 100°F)

1 tbsp sugar

1 envelope regular yeast (2½–3 tsp)

3 cups flour

pinch salt

1½ tsp cinnamon

⅓ cup sugar

¼ cup melted butter

1 large egg

1 large egg white

2 tsp pure vanilla extract

1 cup sultana or golden raisins

1 egg yolk (reserved from preparing the dough)

1½ tbsp water

VANILLA GLAZE

½ cup icing sugar (powdered sugar)

½ tsp vanilla extract

2–3 tsp milk

Here's an Easter specialty that has become a weekend brunch favourite at our house at any time of year. The scent of these cinnamon and vanilla infused buns while baking will wake the entire house in eager anticipation.

I like sultana raisins in mine, but dark or golden raisins or currants are also good. If your family is not fond of dried fruits, these are also exceptionally delicious with chocolate chips substituted for the raisins.

HOT CROSS BUNS

1. Dissolve 1 tbsp of sugar in the warm water. Sprinkle the yeast over the surface. Do not stir. Let stand for 15 minutes.

2. In the bowl of an electric mixer with a dough hook attachment or in a large mixing bowl, mix together the flour, salt, cinnamon, and ⅓ cup sugar.

3. Add the prepared yeast along with the melted butter, 1 egg, 1 egg white (set the second yolk aside for later), and vanilla extract.

4. Knead with the mixer's dough hook for about 5 minutes or mix together with a wooden spoon until the dough comes together, then knead by hand for about 10 minutes. You may need to add a little more flour as you knead, if your dough is too sticky. This is not unusual when making yeast dough of any kind.

5. Knead the raisins into the dough by hand. An electric mixer will crush the raisins, and you want to keep them intact, so gentle hand kneading is best to incorporate raisins into the dough.

6. Cover and let stand in a draft-free, warm place for 30-40 minutes.

tip > Besides being incredibly convenient for recipes like this one, cold proofing in the fridge overnight lets yeast-raised breads and rolls develop better flavour too. Make them in the evening and pop the pan into a large plastic bag, securing the opening with a twist tie. If you like, you can blow air into the bag with a straw before closing it. This maximizes the air space on top of the rising rolls so the dough does not stick to the bag.

7. Grease a 9x13-inch baking pan. Divide the dough into 12 equal pieces and form into balls.

8. Place them in the prepared pan and let rise for about 60 minutes or until about doubled in size.

9. Preheat oven to 350°F.

10. Whisk together the reserved egg yolk and 1½ tbsp water. Brush over the tops of the buns before baking. You need not use it all. This step makes a glossy finish to the tops of the buns.

11. Bake for about 30-35 minutes or a little longer.

12. Remove from pan and let rest on a wire rack for about 15-20 minutes before piping on the vanilla glaze crosses.

VANILLA GLAZE

1. Mix together the icing sugar, vanilla extract, and milk until smooth. You will want this to be quite a stiff glaze so only add enough milk to bring it to a thick consistency.

2. Pipe crosses onto the tops of the warm buns. A Ziploc bag with the corner snipped off works well for this if you do not have a piping bag.

Blueberry Lemon Cornmeal Pancakes

PREP TIME: **10** MINUTES | COOK TIME: **20** MINUTES | MAKES ABOUT **12** LARGE PANCAKES

1½ cups flour

2 tsp baking powder

1 tsp baking soda

pinch salt

⅔ cup yellow cornmeal

4 tbsp sugar

4 tbsp lemon juice

1¾ cups milk

2 egg yolks

¼ cup melted butter

2 tbsp lemon zest, finely chopped

2 tsp vanilla extract

2 egg whites

2 cups blueberries, fresh or frozen

This original photo accompanied the first pancake recipe ever published on *RockRecipes.com* back in the spring of 2008. It has remained the most popular pancake recipe I've posted. Back in the original post, I mentioned that I rarely made pancakes at our house because my ten-year-old daughter, Olivia, had taken on the duties of expert pancake maker. Not much has changed in the years since, but in the times when I still get up early on the weekends, before the kids, I like to whip up a batch of these, my personal favourite pancakes. There are never any complaints from the teenagers, either, when they wake up to the scent of blueberry and lemon wafting up from the kitchen below.

> tip > Don't overmix pancake batter and never re-mix it after the initial mixing; this will deflate the batter and make dense pancakes. Let the batter rest for 5-10 minutes before using. This gives it a chance to relax and let the baking powder do its work. The batter will be lighter and fluffier and so will your pancakes.

1. Sift together the flour, baking powder, baking soda, salt, cornmeal, and sugar. Set aside.

2. Mix together the lemon juice and milk and add to the dry ingredients along with the egg yolks, melted butter, lemon zest, and vanilla extract.

3. Stir together slightly with a wooden spoon, only enough to just form a batter. Lumps are a good thing in pancake batter.

4. Beat 2 egg whites until soft peaks form and fold gently into the batter.

5. Pour batter by ¼ cup measures into a preheated, oiled griddle pan on medium heat or a preheated to 375°F electric griddle pan. Sprinkle each pancake with blueberries. When bubbles start to break the surface of the pancake, it's time to flip them and cook for about another 2 minutes until golden brown.

tip > When cooking pancakes, keep the heat as low as you can and wait for those bubbles. A pancake most often will take more time to cook on the first side than when flipped onto the second side. The best way to ensure a fully cooked pancake is to wait for bubbles to break the surface before flipping. Just take an occasional peek at the bottom to make sure they're not over-browning.

Oatmeal Apple Banana Muffins

PREP TIME: **15** MINUTES | COOK TIME: **25** MINUTES | MAKES **10–12**

1½ cups large rolled oats

1 cup all-purpose or 60% whole-wheat flour

3 tsp baking powder

½ tsp salt

1½ tsp cinnamon

½ tsp nutmeg

2 eggs

4 tbsp vegetable oil

6 tbsp sugar

⅔ cup milk

1 cup mashed ripe banana

1 cup peeled and grated apple (approximately 1 large apple)

This is a very easy to make recipe for moist, delicious breakfast muffins that use a minimum of vegetable oil; although you'll never miss it. The mashed bananas and grated apple keep these muffins particularly moist, and a few seconds in the microwave make them just as good the next day. Plan on making a few extra for early in the week when you're grabbing something to go on the way to work or as a healthier option for the kids lunchboxes.

1.   Preheat oven to 350°F.

2.   Mix together the rolled oats, flour, baking powder, salt, cinnamon, and nutmeg. Set aside.

3.   Beat together the eggs, vegetable oil, and sugar until fluffy.

4.   Blend in the milk.

5.   Fold in the dry ingredients and when the flour is almost incorporated fold in the mashed banana and grated apple.

6.   Do not overmix. Fold in only until the fruit is mixed through the batter.

7.   Spoon into greased or paper-lined muffin tins and bake for 20-25 minutes or until a toothpick inserted in the center comes out clean. Best served warm.

Sour Cream Lemon Scones

PREP TIME: **10** MINUTES | COOK TIME: **18** MINUTES | MAKES **20** SMALL SCONES

These fragrant little lemon scones remind me of a formal afternoon English tea. I think they would fit right in beside the cucumber sandwiches and Victoria sponge cake. Beautifully light and tender, these scones pair particularly well with wild blueberry jam. Some thick cream or clotted cream would also be wonderful to serve with them, especially slathered on in addition to the blueberry jam.

2 cups all-purpose flour

¼ cup sugar

4 tsp baking powder

¼ tsp baking soda

zest of 1 lemon, finely minced

¼ cup + 1 tbsp very cold butter

½ cup sour cream

½ cup milk

1 tsp vanilla extract

1 tbsp water

1 egg

2–3 tbsp turbinado sugar (optional)

pinch salt

1. Preheat oven to 400°F.

2. In a food processor, blend together the flour, sugar, baking powder, baking soda, and lemon zest.

3. Pulse in the butter.

4. Do not over incorporate the butter into the flour. Similar to making a flaky pastry, small pieces of butter should be visible in the flour.

5. Transfer this mixture from the food processor into a large mixing bowl and make a well in the center.

6. Mix together the sour cream, milk, and vanilla. Pour into the well.

7. Working very quickly with a wooden spoon, fold the dry mixture through the buttermilk, only until the flour disappears, then stop immediately. Drop the sticky dough onto a well-floured countertop or bread board. Sprinkle the top of the dough with additional flour as well as flouring your hands to handle the dough. I don't even use a rolling pin for these biscuits; the dough is soft enough to pat out gently with floured hands to a thickness of about ¾ inch. Using a small biscuit cutter, cut the biscuits out and place them, 1½ inches apart, on a parchment paper-lined baking sheet. I recommend an aluminum baking sheet because it tolerates the higher oven temperature without burning the bottom of the biscuits.

8. Whisk together the water and egg and brush lightly over the top of the biscuits. You will only need a little of the egg-wash mixture.

9. Sprinkle with some turbinado sugar if desired.

10. Bake for 13-15 minutes or until the tops are golden brown. Cool on a wire rack.

Apple Cinnamon Sticky Buns

PREP TIME: **30** MINUTES + RISING TIME | COOK TIME: **40** MINUTES | MAKES **12** LARGE BUNS

DOUGH
3 cups all-purpose flour

¼ cup sugar

1 pkg (5 g) instant dry yeast

¼ tsp salt

3 tbsp melted butter

1¼ cups warm milk

2 eggs, slightly beaten

2 tsp vanilla extract

STICKY GLAZE
1 cup brown sugar

½ cup melted butter

DICED APPLE FILLING
1 cup brown sugar

½ cup very soft butter

2 tsp cinnamon

2½ cups diced small apples

VANILLA GLAZE (OPTIONAL)
1 cup icing sugar
(powdered sugar)

½ tsp vanilla extract

2 tbsp milk (approx.)

Like the look of these apple cinnamon sticky buns? They are, in a word, fantastic! Call me immodest, but I have never had a cinnamon roll anywhere that was better than those I bake myself, and this version is a particular favourite of mine. It's a delicious twist on traditional cinnamon buns using diced apples in the filling. A sticky glaze baked at the bottom makes them extra tempting. I only make them when I have a crowd coming over for fear of eating them all myself!

DOUGH

1.   Combine 2 cups of the flour along with the sugar, instant yeast, and salt in a large bowl or in the bowl of a large electric mixer that uses a dough hook.

2.   Add the melted butter, warm milk, eggs, and vanilla extract.

3.   Using a wooden spoon or the regular paddle of your electric mixer beat for 4-5 minutes until the mixture is smooth with no lumps.

4.   If using an electric mixer, switch to the dough hook at this point and begin to slowly incorporate the remaining 1 cup of flour. If not using an electric mixer, keep mixing in the flour gradually until a soft dough forms that leaves the sides of the bowl. You may need to use a little less or a little more flour, this is not uncommon.

5.   Knead the dough for an additional 10 minutes either in the electric mixer or on a bread board or countertop.

6.   Cover dough and leave to rest and rise for 1 hour. Punch the dough down and knead it for a few minutes by hand before letting it rest for another 10 minutes.

7.   Roll the rested dough out into a large rectangle about 12x18 inches.

> note > The rising times provided are approximations. In a warm kitchen, the rolls may rise faster.

STICKY GLAZE

1. Combine the 1 cup brown sugar and ½ cup melted butter in the bottom of the pan before adding the rolls.

DICED APPLE FILLING

1. Combine 1 cup brown sugar, the soft butter and cinnamon to make a paste.

2. Spread this mixture on the rolled-out dough. Evenly sprinkle on the diced apples.

3. Starting at the short side of the rectangle, roll the dough into a log, pinching the dough together to seal at the end of the roll.

4. Cut the roll into 12 equal pieces and place in the bottom of a greased 9x13-inch baking pan.

5. **note** > For Sticky Buns, combine 1 cup brown sugar and ½ cup melted butter in the bottom of the pan before adding the rolls. Invert onto a platter when baked.

6. Cover the baking pan with a clean tea towel and allow the rolls to rise until at least doubled in size, about 60-90 minutes. (I sometimes let them rise in the fridge overnight and pop them into the oven in the morning. I've also frozen them before they rise and take them out of the freezer to rise overnight on the countertop before going to bed.)

7. Preheat oven to 350°F and bake for 30-40 minutes or until the rolls spring back when touched in the middle of the pan. Frost with vanilla glaze if desired.

VANILLA GLAZE (OPTIONAL)

1. Whisk all three ingredients together until smooth, and drizzle over the cinnamon rolls. If the glaze seems too thin, add a little more icing sugar.

Sausage and Garlic Quiche
with Smoked Cheddar Sauce

PREP TIME: **30** MINUTES | COOK TIME: **35** MINUTES | SERVES **6–8**

QUICHE CRUST

½ cup very cold butter cut into small cubes

1¼ cups flour

¼ tsp salt

3–4 tbsp ice water (only enough to make a dough form)

QUICHE FILLING

¾ lb of uncooked loose sausage meat of your choice

3 cloves garlic, minced

6 large or extra-large eggs

¾ cup whipping cream

¼ tsp black pepper

¼ tsp salt

SMOKED CHEDDAR SAUCE

2 tbsp flour

2 tbsp butter

¼ tsp black pepper

1 cup hot milk

salt to taste

1 cup grated smoked cheddar cheese

This recipe has been included in this book more as a base recipe to build on, and to demonstrate technique in achieving a good quiche. Always use the same blind-baking method to avoid a soggy crust and always use the same proportion of eggs to whipping cream to create a firm filling. Other than that, substitute the sausage and garlic for any combination of fresh herbs, onions, grated cheese, crisp bacon, ham, etc. to create your own personal favourite quiche.

QUICHE CRUST

1. Using a food processor or a pastry blender, cut cold butter into the flour and salt until the mixture resembles a coarse meal. Small pieces of butter should still be visible. Pour cold water over the mixture and work in by tossing with a fork until a dough begins to form. Use your hands as little as possible and work the dough as little as possible. Wrap in plastic wrap and place in the refrigerator to rest for a minimum of 20 minutes. You can make your dough the previous day, but make sure you take it out of the fridge for 10 minutes to warm slightly before rolling out.

2. Preheat oven to 375°F.

3. Roll the dough into a 12-inch round and place in the bottom of a 9-inch pie plate. Push the dough edges down the sides, being careful not to stretch the dough at all. Crimp the edge of the dough however you like.

4. You will need to blind bake this bottom crust before adding the filling. Blind baking is essential to ensure the bottom crust does not get soggy. To blind bake a crust, simply place a piece of parchment paper or aluminum foil over the dough and cover the bottom of the pie plate with baking weights. (Marbles, dry beans, peas, rice, or barley work just as well as anything else.)

5. Bake for about 15 minutes. Remove baking weights and parchment (or foil) and bake for an additional 5 minutes. Remove crust from oven and let cool for a few minutes while you prepare the filling.

QUICHE FILLING

1. Reduce the oven heat to 325°F.

2. In a medium-sized sauté pan, fully cook the sausage over medium heat, breaking it up into small pieces about the size of the tip of your little finger. In the last couple of minutes of cooking time, add the minced garlic, sautéing it together with the sausage, just to soften it. Drain any excess fat from the pan. Set aside to cool a little before adding the sausage and garlic to the prepared quiche crust, dispersing it evenly on the bottom.

3. Whisk together the eggs, whipping cream, pepper, and salt very well, and then pour slowly and evenly over the sausage and garlic.

4. Bake for 30-35 minutes or until the center of the quiche has set.

5. Serve with warm Smoked Cheddar Sauce.

SMOKED CHEDDAR SAUCE

1. In a small saucepan, combine and cook the flour, butter, black pepper, and salt for 2 minutes over medium-low heat.

2. Whisking constantly, slowly pour in the hot milk and continue to stir for 2-3 minutes until the sauce thickens slightly.

3. Remove from heat and season with salt to taste, and then add the grated smoked cheddar cheese.

4. Let stand for 1 minute to allow the cheese to melt, then whisk until smooth. Serve over slices of the quiche.

Garlic Parmesan Potato Latkes

PREP TIME: **15** MINUTES | COOK TIME: **10** MINUTES | MAKES **8**

This crispy potato pancake recipe could just as easily have been included in the Side Dishes section of this book because, truth be told, we serve them with many main courses for dinner at our house. The kids just love them, and we've served them with everything from a baked-ham dinner to grilled steak.

Much akin to hash browns, these golden little pancakes make an ideal addition to a weekend brunch as well. I love adding different herb or onion flavours to them, but this garlic and Parmesan version is a particular favourite of mine. I've even served them with poached eggs, thinly sliced fried pastrami and Hollandaise sauce as a unique version of Eggs Benedict. That is a highly recommended serving suggestion.

4 cups grated potato

1 clove garlic, very finely minced

salt and pepper to season

½ cup freshly grated Parmesan

1 beaten egg

3 tbsp flour

canola oil for frying

1. Squeeze as much excess water from the grated potato as possible. Add all the remaining ingredients and toss together until well combined.

2. Heat a ½-inch of canola oil in a large non-stick skillet over medium-low to medium heat.

3. Drop the latke mixture by ½-cup measures into the hot oil, spreading it out to about a ½-inch thickness. Fry until golden brown on one side, then turn and cook until golden brown on the opposite side.

4. Drain on paper towels. Serve with sour cream and chopped green onions.

Raspberry Filled Donut Muffins

¾ cup all-purpose flour

¾ cup cake-and-pastry flour

2 tsp baking powder

½ tsp salt

½ tsp freshly ground nutmeg

¾ cup sugar

1 large egg

¼ cup vegetable oil

¾ cup whipping cream

1 tsp vanilla extract

½ cup raspberry jam

melted butter

icing sugar (powdered sugar)

PREP TIME: **15** MINUTES | COOK TIME: **15** MINUTES

MAKES **8** LARGE OR **12** MINI MUFFINS

These soft, moist cake donut muffins remind me of the little jam-filled donut balls made by local bakeries years ago. They could be found at your local neighbourhood store or supermarket when I was growing up here in Newfoundland. As a kid, I remember thinking I would make them with more jam inside and roll them in powdered sugar too. That childhood memory inspired this variation of cake donut muffins. Although they are still an indulgence, they are baked and not fried like regular donuts. Now you can rationalize having two! These are terrific as lunchbox surprises or as the highlight of your weekend brunch.

1. Preheat oven to 350°F.

2. Sift together the flours, baking powder, salt, and nutmeg. Set aside.

3. In a large mixing bowl, whisk together the sugar and egg until very light in colour.

4. Add the oil and whisk in well then add the whipping cream and vanilla extract until well blended.

5. Fold in the dry ingredients by hand just until the dry ingredients are incorporated into the batter. Do not overmix.

6. Bake for about 13 minutes for mini muffins or 15-18 minutes if your muffins are larger. Watch them carefully, and as soon as a wooden toothpick inserted into the center comes out clean, take them out. It is very easy to overbake mini muffins especially.

7. Let them cool for 10 minutes before removing them from the pan. Cool on a wire rack.

8. When the muffins are cooled, fill a piping bag with about ½ cup raspberry jam. Attach a star tip or other larger open tip to the piping bag.

9. Push the piping bag tip into the center of the muffin. This can be done on the top or side of the muffin. Wiggle the piping bag tip around a little bit to create a cavity before squeezing the piping bag to fill the cavity.

10. When all of your muffins are filled, brush the outsides of the muffins with a little melted butter and roll them in powdered sugar before serving.

Some of the most immediate feedback I received on my original *Rock Recipes* cookbook came from folks who loved the cookie section. The Queen Anne Squares were a particular hit and seemed to be the recipe everyone tried first!

With over 200 cookie recipes published online, it was still difficult to choose selections for this second cookbook . So I've relied on lots of fan favourites to make the choices, and I've added a couple of brand new recipes too. It's a great collection, from tried-and-true traditional to ultimately decadent; I think you'll love them all.

cookies and bars

Turtle Cookies 200

Toasted Coconut Shortbread Cookies 202

Gluten Free Chocolate Pavlova Cookies 204

Strawberry Crumble (or Crumble Bars) 206

Lamingtons 208

Aunt Aggies Peanut Butter Cookies 210

Chocolate Walnut Butter Tart Bars 212

Oreo Caramel Brownie Bombs 214

Homemade Jam Jams 216

Blueberry Lemon Cheesecake Bars 218

Brown Butter Cookies 220

Coconut Shortbread Blueberry Crumble Bars 222

Nutella Swirl Brownies 224

Turtle Cookies

PREP TIME: **20** MINUTES | COOK TIME: **10** MINUTES | MAKES **3** DOZEN

Pecans, caramel, and chocolate come together in an absolutely winning combination in this Turtle Cookies recipe. That combination is why everybody loves those gorgeous Turtle chocolates and why Turtle cheesecake is such a popular dessert menu item in restaurants. Inspired by those great little confections, I set out to make a cookie version that would be worthy of the name.

I can report that all testers of these cookies declare them to be amazing. A double chocolate-chip cookie gets rolled in pecans and topped with a soft chewy caramel candy. It then bakes to crispy, chewy perfection. It's surely destined to become one of your household's signature cookie recipes.

2½ cups flour

½ cup very good quality cocoa

1 tsp salt

1 tsp baking soda

1 cup butter

1 cup light brown sugar

1 cup sugar

2 eggs

2 tsp vanilla extract

12 oz semisweet chocolate chips (about 1½ cups)

1 cup chopped pecans

3 dozen individually wrapped caramel candies

1.   Preheat oven to 350°F.

2.   In a medium-sized bowl, whisk together flour, cocoa, salt, and baking soda. Set aside.

3.   In a large bowl, cream together the butter and sugars until light and fluffy. Add the eggs, one at a time, beating thoroughly after each addition. Add the vanilla and beat for an additional minute.

4.   Add the flour mixture to the creamed butter mixture. Mix only enough to incorporate flour. Do not overmix. Fold in the chocolate chips.

5.   Roll into 1-inch balls and dunk one half of the ball into the chopped pecans.

6.   Place the balls on a parchment-lined baking sheet 3 inches apart with the side dunked in pecans facing upward. Press down slightly.

7.   Gently push one caramel candy halfway into the center of each cookie ball.

8.   Bake for 10-12 minutes. Do not overbake or the cookies will be brittle.

9.   Cool for 10 minutes on the baking sheet before removing to a wire rack to cool thoroughly. You can drizzle the tops of the cookies when they've cooled with melted chocolate, but that's completely optional.

Toasted Coconut Shortbread Cookies

PREP TIME: **20** MINUTES | COOK TIME: **20** MINUTES | MAKES **3–4** DOZEN

2 cups dried fine-cut coconut,
lightly toasted

2 cups butter at room temperature

1 cup icing sugar
(powdered sugar)

1 tsp vanilla extract

1 tsp coconut extract

3 cups flour

½ cup cornstarch

Buttery shortbread is one of life's simple pleasures, and the toasted coconut in this recipe adds one more layer of flavour to this cookie classic. I also call these the "Nancy Shortbread Cookies." Nancy is a friend and former work colleague who is a dedicated lover of anything coconut. When planning a visit to my old office at the university last Christmas, I made these cookies to bring along. As the most obsessed coconut worshipper I know, this recipe quickly got her unequivocal stamp of approval, so they're certain to please the coconut lover in your life too.

1. Preheat the oven to 350°F.

2. Toast the coconut by spreading it in a 9x13-inch baking pan and baking for 10-15 minutes or so. Stir it and spread evenly again halfway through the toasting time. Set the toasted coconut aside.

3. Cream together the butter and icing sugar very well until very smooth and creamy. No lumps of butter should be visible.

4. Blend in the vanilla and coconut extracts.

5. Sift together the flour and cornstarch then blend slowly into the creamed mixture until a soft dough forms.

6. Blend the coconut through the dough.

7. Split dough into 2 equal portions and roll each one into a log shape about 1½-2 inches in diameter.

8. Wrap the dough logs in plastic wrap and chill for a couple of hours at least.

9. You can freeze one of the cookie-dough portions for later if you like.

10. This dough will also last in the fridge for 3-4 days, so you can bake a few at a time and enjoy them fresh from the oven if you like.

11. After the dough has chilled, preheat the oven again to 350°F.

12. Line cookie sheets with parchment paper.

13. Using a very sharp knife, cut slices of the dough to about ¼-inch thickness or perhaps a tad less.

14. Place the cookies on the parchment paper at ½-inch apart and bake for 15-20 minutes or until they just start to turn brown at the edges.

15. Let cool for 10 minutes on the pan before transferring them to a wire rack to cool completely. Store in an airtight container.

16. These cookies will freeze quite well for several weeks.

Gluten Free Chocolate Pavlova Cookies

PREP TIME: **10** MINUTES | COOK TIME: **15** MINUTES | MAKES ABOUT **18** LARGE COOKIES

Whether you bake gluten free or not, you'll never throw out leftover egg whites again when you discover these decadent Gluten Free Chocolate Pavlova Cookies. They have crispy edges with a soft, slightly chewy, melt-in-your-mouth center and plenty of indulgent chocolate flavour.

3 cups icing sugar (powdered sugar), measured and then sifted

⅔ cup cocoa, measured and then sifted

2 tsp cornstarch

pinch salt

4 large egg whites

1 tsp vanilla extract

½ tsp plain white vinegar

1 cup chocolate chips

1. Preheat oven to 350°F.

2. Icing sugar, salt, and cocoa are prone to clumping, so it's important to sift them through a sieve before using them in this recipe.

3. Sift together the icing sugar, cocoa, cornstarch, and salt.

4. Mix in the egg whites until smooth.

5. Blend in the vanilla extract and vinegar until smooth, and then fold in the chocolate chips.

6. Line a couple of cookie sheets with parchment paper or silicone liners.

7. Spoon the cookie batter by rounded teaspoons onto the prepared cookie sheets, about 2-3 inches apart. These spread quite a bit, so give them plenty of room. (You can sprinkle on a few extra chocolate chips at this point if you like. It makes them look even more appealing when baked.)

8. Bake for approximately 15 minutes until the cookies have a crackled appearance at the edges and might still look very slightly shiny at the center. It is best to do a test bake of a couple of cookies to get the baking time right.

9. These cookies will be very hot and soft when they come out of the oven, so be sure to let them cool completely on the pan for about 15-20 minutes before transferring them to a wire rack to cool completely.

cookie baking tips

> It's practically impossible to write a standard baking time into a chewy cookie recipe because of differences in the pans being used and variations in actual temperatures between ovens. The difference between a chewy cookie and an overbaked cookie can be as little as a minute in many ovens, so I always make two general suggestions:

1. Be sure the oven is fully preheated, then get the cookie sheet into the oven and close the door as fast as possible so the heat will come back up quickly. This helps each pan of cookies to bake consistently.

2. With any new cookie recipe, bake a test batch of only 2 or 3 cookies to get the oven timing perfect before baking the rest of the batch. Be sure to make a note in the margins of the recipe of the exact time they were in the oven for the next time you bake the cookies.

Strawberry Crumble (or Crumble Bars)

PREP TIME: **10** MINUTES | COOK TIME: **45** MINUTES | MAKES ABOUT **18** LARGE COOKIES

What's better than a great crumble recipe? A crumble recipe that can be cut into cookie bars too! This very simple recipe does double duty. It is a delicious buttery crumble recipe that uses just a few simple ingredients to makes a terrific dessert all on its own or with a scoop of good quality vanilla ice cream. Any leftovers can be cut into bar cookies and served cold for the kids' lunchboxes. I can't guarantee the leftovers though, so to be safe, make two batches!

3 cups flour

1 cup sugar

2 tsp baking powder

1½ cups cold butter cut in cubes

2 tsp vanilla extract or the seeds of 1 vanilla pod

2½ cups high fruit content strawberry jam

1. Preheat oven to 350°F.

2. Lightly grease a 9x13-inch baking pan and line with parchment paper.

3. In a food processor, mix together the flour, sugar, and baking powder.

4. Pulse in the cold butter and vanilla until crumbly.

5. If you don't have a food processor, you can simply rub the butter through the dry ingredients with your hands. This is a pretty simple, fail-safe recipe.

6. Press half of the crumb mixture into the bottom of the prepared pan then spread on the strawberry jam. Use homemade or a good quality, whole-fruit jam and not a pectin-based, jelly-type jam.

7. Press the remaining crumb mixture together in your hands and break off small pieces, scattering them evenly over the jam layer.

8. Bake for 40-50 minutes or until light golden brown on top.

9. Serve warm with ice cream or chill and cut into bars.

> tip > The strawberry jam is important in this recipe. If you don't have homemade, buy a high-quality jarred jam that has a higher proportion of fruit to sugar. A jelly type jam with high pectin and sugar does not work as well.

Lamingtons

PREP TIME: **20** MINUTES + FREEZING TIME | COOK TIME: **35** MINUTES | MAKES **24** SQUARES

CAKE SQUARES

1¼ cups sifted all-purpose flour

1½ cups sifted cake flour

½ tsp baking soda

1½ tsp baking powder

1 tsp salt

1½ cups sugar

⅔ cup vegetable oil

⅓ cup vegetable shortening at room temperature

3 tbsp good-quality vanilla extract

3 large eggs

1½ cups buttermilk

CHOCOLATE SYRUP AND COCONUT

1 cup cocoa

1¼ cups white sugar

1½ cups water

1 tsp vanilla extract

4 cups (approx.) dried shredded coconut

I first posted this recipe on *RockRecipes.com* as Chocolate Coconut Cake Squares, an attempt at recreating a treat from my childhood that I remembered fondly. My grandmother made them, but I had never seen a recipe for them that I remember. This version, and a Jell-O-dipped one, always seemed to be served at parties when I was very young, and I just loved them.

The first day I posted this recipe, I heard from dozens of Australians informing me that these are an Aussie favourite called Lamingtons, reportedly named for Lord Lamington, Governor of Queensland at the turn of the 20th century. How this recipe became popular in Newfoundland in the 70s, or possibly earlier, is a mystery to me. I received so many responses from Australia, New Zealand, and even from places like Hong Kong and Singapore, that I updated the name on my blog to reflect their heritage.

CAKE SQUARES

1. Preheat oven to 325°F.

2. Grease a 9×13-inch baking pan and line with parchment paper.

3. Sift together the flours, baking soda, baking powder, salt, and sugar. Set aside.

4. In the bowl of an electric mixer, beat together the vegetable oil, shortening, and vanilla. Beat well at high speed with whisk attachment until light and fluffy.

5. Beat the eggs in one at a time.

6. Fold in the dry ingredients alternately with the buttermilk.

7. I always add dry ingredients in 3 divisions and liquid ingredients in 2 divisions. It is very important to begin and end the additions with the dry ingredients. Do not overmix the batter. As soon as it has no lumps in the batter, pour into the prepared 9×13-inch pan.

8. Bake 30-35 minutes or until a wooden toothpick inserted in the center comes out clean. Allow the cake to cool completely in the pan.

9. Wrap the pan in plastic wrap and place in the freezer until the cake is completely frozen.

10. When frozen, lift the cake out of the pan using the parchment paper as an aid and cut it into 24 squares. Return to the freezer until ready to dip in the chocolate syrup and coconut.

CHOCOLATE SYRUP AND COCONUT

1. Whisk together the cocoa and sugar. This helps to remove any small lumps from the cocoa.

2. Add the water and vanilla.

3. Bring to a slow rolling boil and cook for 5-6 minutes. The syrup should thicken slightly but will still be quite thin.

4. Cool completely to room temperature.

5. Working quickly, dip the frozen cake cubes into the syrup. You don't want to soak too much syrup into the cake.

6. Quickly roll the soaked cake into the coconut and place on a parchment-lined baking sheet to dry.

7. Store in airtight plastic containers. If you are freezing the dessert squares, put them back in the freezer right away.

Aunt Aggies Peanut Butter Cookies

PREP TIME: **10** MINUTES | COOK TIME: **12** MINUTES | MAKES **18**

This recipe was my favourite cookie as a kid and one of the very first that I learned to bake. The recipe came from my Aunt Martha Thompson, who was always called Aunt Aggie in our family circles; although I have no idea why. I was totally in love with these peanut-butter cookies, and no doubt about it, Aunt Aggie always made the best. I can't venture a guess as to how many of these I ate with a tall glass of cold milk during my formative years, but they always bring back very fond memories of childhood for me.

The tradition continues to the next generation as my daughter, Olivia, the other peanut-butter-cookie fan in the household, makes these on a regular basis now. She was the one who made the batch in this photo too; yet another arena in which she is destined to surpass my skills!

½ cup butter

½ cup peanut butter

½ cup white sugar

½ cup brown sugar

1 egg

1 tsp vanilla extract

1¼ cups flour

1 tsp baking soda

pinch salt

1. Preheat oven to 350°F.

2. Cream together the butter, peanut butter, white sugar, and brown sugar until well light and fluffy.

3. Beat in the egg and vanilla extract.

4. Sift together the flour, baking soda, and salt.

5. Fold the dry ingredients into the creamed mixture until a soft dough forms.

6. Roll the dough into 1-inch balls and place on a parchment-lined baking sheet 2-3 inches apart.

7. Press down slightly with a fork (or with the bottom of a water glass dipped in flour as were the cookies shown in the photo).

8. Bake for 12 minutes until golden brown at the edges. Be careful not to overbake, or the cookies will be brittle. The cookies may need a minute more or less in your oven. Bake a few as a test and let them cool before trying them. Refrigerate the dough between batches.

tip > For those dealing with peanut allergies in their family, I have had recent successes substituting other nut butters like cashew or almond as well as toasted soy butter in this recipe. They were all delicious.

Chocolate Walnut Butter Tart Bars

PREP TIME: 20 MINUTES | **COOK TIME: 40** MINUTES | MAKES ABOUT **24**

I'll admit we do a lot of baking around our house, but I limit my intake of the sweets and share the bounty liberally with friends and neighbours. One of the baked goodies I find hardest to resist is a sweet, sticky, delicious butter tart, and these butter tart bars are very reminiscent of this Canadian classic pastry. This recipe has the background taste of a legendarily good Canadian butter tart with the added crunch of toasty walnuts and luscious chocolate. It's a perfect recipe for the holiday freezer or to enjoy at any time of the year.

BOTTOM LAYER

1 cup flour

¼ cup brown sugar

½ cup salted butter

TOP LAYER

1½ cups brown sugar

2 eggs

¾ cup coarsely chopped walnuts

2 tsp vanilla extract

pinch salt

½ tsp baking powder

1 cup chocolate chips

BOTTOM LAYER

1. Preheat oven to 350°F.

2. Using your hands, rub together the ingredients for the bottom layer until well blended and crumbly.

3. Press evenly into the bottom of an 8- or 9-inch square pan that has been lightly greased and lined with parchment paper. Bake for 15 minutes while you prepare the topping.

TOP LAYER

1. Mix together well all the ingredients for the top layer and pour over baked base.

2. Reduce oven to 325°F and return to the oven for 20-25 minutes.

3. Allow the cookie bars to cool completely before cutting. These will cut best after they have been refrigerated.

Oreo Caramel Brownie Bombs

PREP TIME: **45** MINUTES | COOK TIME: **35** MINUTES | MAKES **25** SQUARES

CHOCOLATE CHIP COOKIE BASE

½ cup butter

1 cup brown sugar

1 egg

1 tsp vanilla extract

1 cup + 3 tbsp flour

1 tsp baking powder

⅛ tsp baking soda

½ cup chocolate chips

18 Oreo cookies, broken into quarters

24 soft caramel candies

BROWNIE BATTER

¾ cup all-purpose flour

2 tbsp cocoa powder

¼ tsp salt

½ cup butter

5 squares unsweetened chocolate

¾ cup granulated sugar

¼ cup light-brown sugar

3 large eggs

1 tsp vanilla extract

CHOCOLATE GANACHE

⅓ cup whipping cream

1⅓ cups chocolate chips

When I first posted a photo of this recipe on the *Rock Recipes* Facebook page, I asked for name suggestions for this ultimately decadent cookie bar. Let's just say that some of the suggestions awakened certain primal urges in people, and you wouldn't want to enter the titles into a search engine, that's for sure!

I was going to write my own description here, but I'll leave that to one fan who wrote this brilliant endorsement: "A coworker brought these in to the office yesterday. May I just say, they are the most delicious brownies I've ever had in my life, and I'm an almost 50-yr-old passionate foodie with a lifelong chocolate addiction. They're chewy, crunchy, gooey and soooo very chocolaty. Thank you for sharing this fantastic recipe!"

Is there really anything I could add to that?

CHOCOLATE CHIP COOKIE BASE

1. Preheat oven to 350°F (325°F if using glass bakeware).

2. Lightly grease a 9x9-inch baking pan and line with parchment paper.

3. Cream the butter and brown sugar until light and fluffy.

4. Add the egg and vanilla extract and beat well.

5. Sift together the flour, baking powder, and baking soda.

6. Add dry ingredients to the creamed mixture, folding to combine well. Fold in the chocolate chips.

7. Spread in the prepared baking pan and bake for 15 minutes.

8. Prepare the brownie batter while the base is in the oven so that it is at the ready.

9. Remove the base from oven and immediately sprinkle evenly with the Oreo pieces and caramel candies.

BROWNIE BATTER

1. Sift together flour, cocoa, and salt.

2. Melt together butter and unsweetened chocolate over low heat.

3. Remove from heat and cool to lukewarm.

4. Add sugar, eggs, and vanilla. Stir very well until sugars are dissolved.

5. Pour batter over the Oreo pieces and caramel candies, return to the oven and bake for an additional 15-20 minutes or until the surface of the brownie batter is no longer glossy. Cool completely.

6. Top with a drizzle of chocolate ganache if desired. Cut into 2-inch squares.

CHOCOLATE GANACHE

1. Scald the whipping cream almost to boiling. This can be done quickly in the microwave.

2. Pour the scalded cream over the chocolate chips.

3. Let stand for 5 minutes then stir until smooth.

4. Spoon the ganache into a Ziploc bag, and using sharp scissors, snip a small corner of the bag off and pipe a thin stream of the ganache in a continuous circular pattern over the squares.

Homemade Jam Jams

PREP TIME: **15** MINUTES + CHILLING TIME | COOK TIME: **15** MINUTES

MAKES **12** LARGE OR **24** SMALL COOKIES

Jam Jams from Purity Factories are an undeniable Newfoundland institution. They are soft, almost cake-like, molasses cookies that are sandwiched together with jam. They have been produced from the long-standing factory on Blackmarsh Road here in St. John's for decades and have never diminished in popularity.

Here's my recipe version of the local, molasses-and-jam cookie classic. If you can get your hands on some of Purity Factories Partridgeberry and Apple Jam, it makes the ideal filling for these scrumptious sandwich cookies. They make terrific little soft molasses cookies all on their own too, without the jam centers, especially with a hot cup of tea. Enjoy these however you like them best.

2¾ cups all-purpose flour

¼ tsp salt

2 tsp baking powder

¾ cup lightly packed dark brown sugar

¾ cup butter

1 egg

½ cup molasses

1 tbsp partridgeberry apple jam per cookie (or your favourite jelly or jam)

1. Sift together the flour, salt, and baking powder and set aside.

2. Cream the brown sugar with the butter.

3. Beat in the egg.

4. Beat in the molasses.

5. Stir in the dry ingredients until a soft dough forms.

6. Chill dough for several hours or overnight before rolling it out on a well-floured board and cutting out 3-inch circles. Cut a ½-inch circle out of the center of half of the rolled out cookies.

7. Preheat oven to 350°F and bake on a parchment-lined baking sheet for about 10-12 minutes.

8. Flip the bottom halves of the cookies over (those without the center holes) on the cookie sheet, and while the cookies are still hot, spoon 1 tbsp partridgeberry apple jam per cookie (or your favourite jelly) onto the middle of the flipped cookies and spread it out slightly but not to the edges.

9. Use the cookies with the circle cutouts as the tops of the sandwich cookies and press down slightly.

10. Return to the oven for 2-3 minutes. This step helps the jam stick better, but you can just cool them and put them together cold too, though they tend to be a little messier.

11. Cool on a wire rack.

12. Alternatively, you can just roll the dough into 1-inch balls, roll the balls in plain sugar, and bake them on a parchment-lined cookie sheet for about 12 minutes at 350°F. You can make sandwich cookies out of them or serve them as soft molasses cookies just as they are.

Blueberry Lemon Cheesecake Bars

PREP TIME: **20** MINUTES | COOK TIME: **35** MINUTES | MAKES **24** SQUARES

1½ cups graham crumbs

¼ cup melted butter

3 tbsp sugar

8 oz cream cheese (1 cup)

⅓ cup sugar

1–2 tsp vanilla extract

1 egg

⅓ cup whipping cream

zest of 1 small lemon (or ½ large), finely minced

1 cup fresh or frozen blueberries

When you want all that luscious cheesecake flavour and creamy texture without making an entire huge cheesecake, these perfectly portioned little bites of lemon blueberry cheesecake are just the thing.

These are a quick way to make small servings of a delicious cheesecake, which I especially like to have on hand in the freezer during the holiday season. I either pre-cut them into bars and freeze them in airtight containers with each one nestled inside a paper muffin tin liner or I freeze an entire batch, uncut, in case I need larger servings as a decadent dessert for unexpected dinner guests. Either way, you will always be prepared to serve something utterly delicious to serve family or guests.

1. Preheat oven to 300°F.

2. Lightly grease a 9×9-inch baking pan and line it with parchment paper.

3. Mix together the graham crumbs, melted butter, and 3 tbsp sugar and press into the bottom of the prepared pan.

4. Beat together the cream cheese, ⅓ cup sugar, and vanilla extract until smooth.

5. Add the egg and beat for 1 minute.

6. Blend in the whipping cream along with the lemon zest.

7. Pour over the prepared crust.

8. Sprinkle the blueberries evenly over the cheesecake batter.

9. Bake for 25-35 minutes until the center sets.

10. To ensure even baking, you can place the baking pan into a larger baking pan and fill halfway up with boiling water. This may slow down the cooking process and require a little extra baking time, but the cheesecake will bake more evenly from the edges to the center.

11. Cool completely before cutting into bars and serving. Store in the refrigerator or freeze until needed.

Brown Butter Cookies

PREP TIME: **20** MINUTES | COOK TIME: **15** MINUTES | MAKES **3** DOZEN

1 cup salted butter

2 cups brown sugar

1 tbsp vanilla extract

2 eggs

¼ cup milk

2¾ cups flour

1 tsp baking soda

With only 7 ingredients, these cookies are simple perfection. Crispy at the edges, chewy at the center, and full of intense caramel flavour, these uncomplicated cookies may just become your new sweet addiction. The secret, of course, is browning the butter before making the cookie dough. This method maximizes the final, intensely buttery, caramel flavour. As soon as you smell the heavenly fragrance as the vanilla extract hits the brown butter and brown sugar in the mixing bowl, you won't dare call this a "plain" cookie!

1. You will need to make the brown butter in advance and let it cool completely. To brown butter, just melt the 1 cup of butter in a small saucepan over medium heat and watch it carefully until the colour turns light golden brown. Pour it off immediately into a heat-proof measuring cup, leaving the sediment behind. Allow the brown butter to cool to room temperature and solidify. This should produce about ¾ cup of brown butter.

2. Cream the brown butter with the brown sugar and vanilla extract until light and fluffy.

3. Add the eggs, one at a time, and beat well for 2-3 minutes, then beat in the milk.

4. Sift together the flour and baking soda, and then fold into the creamed mixture until all the flour is incorporated and a soft dough forms.

5. Cover or wrap the dough and chill for at least 30-60 minutes.

6. Preheat oven to 350°F.

7. Roll the dough into 2-inch balls. I weighed 2-ounce portions of dough to make large cookies as shown in the photograph.

8. Place the prepared dough balls onto a parchment-lined baking sheet about 2 inches apart and flatten them slightly with the heel of your hand or with the bottom of a drinking glass.

9. Bake for 15 minutes or until they just start to turn brown at the bottom edges.

10. Let them cool on the baking pan for 5 minutes before transferring to a wire rack to cool completely.

11. Store in airtight containers. These cookies also freeze well.

Coconut Shortbread
Blueberry Crumble Bars

BLUEBERRY FILLING

3 cups fresh or frozen blueberries

⅔ cup sugar

1 rounded tbsp cornstarch

1 oz cold water

COCONUT SHORTBREAD CRUMBLE

1 cup cold butter cut in cubes

1½ tsp vanilla extract

2 cups flour

⅔ cup sugar

1¼ tsp baking powder

⅔ cup dried medium-cut coconut

A successful coconut shortbread cookie recipe, which was a big hit on my Christmas baking list this past year, inspired this cookie-bar recipe. Crumble cookie bars of all types have always been popular in our family, but I'd never seen a blueberry version that incorporated coconut, so I thought what better occasion to try it than the chance to add it to a new cookbook. They were such a success that Spouse quickly whisked them away to the freezer only an hour after we first cut them. We both found them irresistible.

BLUEBERRY FILLING

1. In a small saucepan, simmer the blueberries and sugar slowly for about 20 minutes. You want to cook off some of the liquid in the filling and intensify the flavour of the berries.

2. Dissolve the cornstarch in the water and add to the simmering berries, stirring constantly. Cook for 1 minute longer. Remove from heat and let cool completely to room temperature. I often make the filling in advance and store it, covered, in the fridge overnight.

COCONUT SHORTBREAD CRUMBLE

1. Preheat oven to 350°F.

2. Lightly grease a 9x9-inch baking pan and line with parchment paper.

3. In a food processor mix together the flour, sugar, and baking powder.

4. Pulse in the cold butter and vanilla until crumbly.

5. If you don't have a food processor, you can simply rub the butter through the dry ingredients with your hands. This is a pretty simple, fail-safe recipe.

6. When completely crumbly, mix in the dried coconut by hand.

7. Press half of the crumb mixture into the bottom of the prepared pan, then spread on the blueberry filling.

8. Press the remaining crumb mixture together in your hands and break off small pieces, scattering them evenly over the filling layer.

9. Bake for 45-50 minutes or until light golden brown on top.

Nutella Swirl Brownies

1 cup butter

2¼ cups sugar

⅔ cup Nutella

1 cup cocoa powder

1 tsp baking powder

½ tsp salt

4 large or extra-large eggs

1 tsp vanilla extract

1½ cups flour

¾ cup semisweet chocolate chips

⅓ cup Nutella

PREP TIME: 20 MINUTES | COOK TIME: 40 MINUTES
MAKES 30–36

These indulgent brownies are soft, chocolaty, have chewy edges, and are swirled with Nutella in the batter. Without a doubt, these are some of the best brownies I have ever tried. Brownie lovers seem to be divided into two groups, the edge lovers like me and the center-cut lovers who like the middle best. This recipe will please everyone because the edges get chewy and delicious while the center is oh-so fudgy. The swirl of Nutella through the batter makes them even better. A tall glass of cold milk and one of these beauties would make any kid extremely happy. They make the start of some pretty incredible brownie sundaes too!

1. Preheat oven to 350°F.

2. Lightly grease a 9×13-inch baking pan and line with parchment paper.

3. In a small saucepan melt the butter.

4. Remove from the heat and stir in the sugar. Dissolving the sugar in the butter is an essential step. You want to pinch the mixture between your fingers and make sure you can't feel any sugar grains; this step helps to create the soft, chewy, fudgy texture of the brownies. If you need to return the mixture to the heat to get the sugar dissolved, only place it on the burner over medium heat for 30 seconds at a time and stir again. It is important that the mixture is not too hot when you add the Nutella, so cool it down for 15 minutes or so if you have to before moving on to the next step.

5. When the sugar is dissolved, stir in the ⅔ cup of Nutella until smooth.

6. Sift together the cocoa powder, baking powder, and salt (not the flour) and add it to the sugar, butter, and Nutella mixture along with the eggs and vanilla.

7. Using an electric mixer on low, mix until smooth.

8. Finally, fold in the flour and chocolate chips by hand.

9. Spread the batter evenly in the pan.

10. Take an additional ⅓ cup of Nutella and drop it by the teaspoonful all over the surface of the batter. Using the handle of a wooden spoon, swirl the Nutella through the batter.

11. Bake for 40 minutes. Let cool in the pan before cutting and serving.

Over the past eight years, since I started *RockRecipes.com*, I feel like I've been part of thousands of celebrations around the world because someone somewhere has baked one of my cake recipes to mark an occasion. Many of the questions I answer online are about cake recipes or about which cake would be good for a particular occasion. Some of the most popular choices, like Lemon Velvet Cake, have seen millions of hits online and have no doubt been served at thousands of birthdays and anniversaries. I hope you find one here to make your next celebration even just a little bit more special.

cakes

Classic Victoria Sandwich Cake 228

Lemon Velvet Cake 230

Hummingbird Cake 232

One Bowl Gingerbread Cake *with* Mango Vanilla Jam 234

Cherry Pecan Cake 236

Sticky Toffee Banana Cake *with* Cream Cheese Frosting 238

The Ultimate Strawberries *and* Cream Cake 240

Spice Velvet Cake 242

Too Tall Neapolitan Cake 244

Brandied Peach Shortcake 248

Double Chocolate Truffle Cake 250

Classic Victoria Sandwich Cake

PREP TIME: **20** MINUTES | COOK TIME: **25** MINUTES | SERVES **10–12**

Favoured by Queen Victoria herself at afternoon tea, this very simple cake is much akin to pound cake in its ingredient proportions, using an equal weight of the basic four ingredients: flour, sugar, butter, and eggs. Don't skimp on a generous layer of jam at the center either. Raspberry is traditional, but any favourite jam will do. Put together some cucumber or cress sandwiches, bake some scones or Jammie Dodgers and indulge in afternoon tea with a generous slice of this simply perfect little cake.

1¼ cups **flour**

1 tsp **baking powder**

pinch **salt**

¾ cup **butter**

⅔ cup **sugar**

3 large **eggs**

2 tsp **vanilla extract**

1½–2 cups **good quality raspberry jam**

powdered sugar for garnish

1. Preheat oven to 350°F. Grease and flour two 8-inch cake pans and line the bottoms with parchment paper.

2. Sift together the flour, baking powder, and salt and set aside.

3. Cream together the butter and sugar very well for several minutes until very light and fluffy.

4. Add the eggs, one at a time, beating for about a minute or two after each addition. Beat in the vanilla extract.

5. Finally, carefully and as lightly as possible, fold in the flour mixture in two equal portions. Divide the batter evenly between the two cake pans and bake for about 25 minutes until the middle of the cakes springs back when pressed lightly and a wooden toothpick inserted in the center comes out clean. Cool the cakes in the pans for a few minutes before turning them out onto a wire rack to cool completely.

6. Fill the middle of the cake with a generous amount of raspberry jam, and using a metal sieve dust the top of the cake with plenty of powdered sugar.

Lemon Velvet Cake

PREP TIME: **20** MINUTES | COOK TIME: **35** MINUTES | SERVES **12–16**

This lemon cake is a perfectly moist and tender crumbed cake with a lemony buttercream frosting. The recipe came about as I tried to develop a cake that had a softer, less dense texture than many homemade cake recipes. This unique method, the result of many experiments, was so successful that it turned into an entire series of recipes on *RockRecipes.com*, including white, orange, and chocolate versions. Fans of my blog love this cake, and it is now in our top 25 recipes of all time, having had hundreds of thousands of views on the website. It was also the cake recipe most requested to be included in this cookbook, so there is no doubt that it would make the ideal birthday cake for the lemon lover in your life.

LEMON VELVET CAKE

1¼ cups sifted **all-purpose flour**

1½ cups sifted **cake flour**

½ tsp **baking soda**

1½ tsp **baking powder**

1 tsp **salt**

1½ cups **sugar**

⅔ cup **vegetable oil**

⅓ cup **vegetable shortening** at room temperature

1 tsp good quality **vanilla extract**

2 tsp **pure lemon extract**

3 **large eggs**

zest of 1 **large** or 2 **small lemons**, grated and finely chopped

1½ cups **buttermilk**

BUTTERCREAM FROSTING

8 cups **icing sugar** (powdered sugar)

2 cups **unsalted butter**

1 tsp minced **lemon zest** (optional)

1 tsp **pure lemon extract**

4 tbsp **milk** (approx.)

LEMON VELVET CAKE

1. Preheat oven to 325°F. Grease and flour two 9-inch round cake pans and line the bottom with 2 circles of parchment paper. Sift together both flours, baking soda, baking powder, salt, and sugar. Set aside.

2. In the bowl of an electric mixer, beat together the vegetable oil, shortening, vanilla, and lemon extract. Beat well at high speed with whisk attachment until light and fluffy.

3. Beat the eggs in one at a time.

4. Fold in the lemon zest.

5. Fold in the dry ingredients alternately with the buttermilk.

6. I always add dry ingredients in 3 divisions and liquid ingredients in 2 divisions. It is very important to begin and end the additions with the dry ingredients. Do not overmix the batter. As soon as it has no lumps in the batter, pour into the 2 prepared cake pans.

7. Bake for 30-35 minutes or until a wooden toothpick inserted in the center comes out clean. Allow the cake to cool in the pans for 10 minutes before turning out onto wire racks to cool completely.

BUTTERCREAM FROSTING

1. Mix together the icing sugar, butter, and lemon zest until it becomes sort of crumbly.

2. Add the lemon extract and a little of the milk.

3. Beat until smooth and fluffy, adding only enough milk to bring the frosting to a creamy spreadable consistency.

4. Fill and frost the cake.

HUMMINGBIRD CAKE

3 cups **flour**

½ tsp **salt**

1 tsp **baking soda**

1½ tsp **baking powder**

2 tsp **cinnamon**

1 tsp **nutmeg**

1 cup **white sugar**

1 cup **brown sugar**

3 **eggs**

1 cup **canola oil**

2 tsp **vanilla extract**

1 tsp **butterscotch flavouring**
(optional)

1 cup **crushed pineapple**

1 cup roughly chopped **toasted pecans**

3 **medium-size bananas**, ripe but firm and cut in quarters lengthways and diced

CREAM CHEESE FROSTING

1 cup **cream cheese**

½ cup **butter**

½ cup **shortening**

2 tsp **vanilla extract**

8 cups **icing sugar**

2–4 tbsp **milk**

Hummingbird Cake

PREP TIME: 20 MINUTES | COOK TIME: 40 MINUTES
SERVES 12–16

Hummingbird Cake is a close cousin to the carrot cake but with bananas, pineapple, and crunchy pecans as the stand-out flavours. Like carrot cake, though, it still loves to be paired with luscious cream-cheese frosting.

This is a very old and popular dessert cake in the southern states, and one of my favourite things about it is the nutty crunch of the toasted pecans in the mildly spiced, moist cake. That will not surprise those of you who know my lust for pecan pie. Pecans and bananas are a naturally good combination, and although you could choose to mash the bananas in this recipe, I like to dice them into small pieces and fold them into the batter for sweet pockets of banana all throughout the cake. It may seem like overkill to add crushed pineapple to this cake, and you may be concerned about muddling the flavours, but trust me, it works... and deliciously well.

HUMMINGBIRD CAKE

1. Preheat oven to 350°. Grease two 9-inch round cake pans and line bottoms with parchment paper. Grease the paper as well and dust the pans lightly with flour.

2. Sift together flour, salt, baking soda, baking powder, cinnamon, and nutmeg. Set aside.

3. Mix the sugars, eggs, oil, vanilla extract, and butterscotch flavouring until light and fluffy. Stir in the crushed pineapple.

4. Fold in the dry ingredients until not quite completely mixed through. Finally add in the chopped nuts and chopped bananas, folding gently until the last of the flour has been fully incorporated.

5. Divide equally between the 2 prepared cake pans and bake for about 30-35 minutes or until a toothpick inserted in the center comes out clean. Cool in the pans for 10 minutes before turning the cakes out onto a wire rack to cool completely. Frost with Cream Cheese Frosting.

CREAM CHEESE FROSTING

1. Combine all ingredients together and beat until smooth. Add only enough milk to bring the icing to a creamy spreadable consistency.

2. Like carrot cake, because of the frosting, this cake should be stored in the refrigerator. I like to take it out 30 minutes or so before serving to let the frosting soften a little.

One Bowl Gingerbread Cake
with Mango Vanilla Jam

PREP TIME: **30** MINUTES | COOK TIME: **40** MINUTES | SERVES **12–16**

GINGERBREAD CAKE

1 cup sugar

2½ cups all-purpose flour

3 tbsp powdered ginger

1 tsp cinnamon

½ tsp ground cloves

2 tsp baking powder

1 tsp baking soda

½ tsp salt

2 eggs

1 cup soured milk

½ cup fancy or light molasses (not cooking molasses or blackstrap molasses)

½ cup vegetable oil

1 tsp vanilla extract

1 tbsp freshly grated ginger root (optional)

MANGO VANILLA JAM

1 vanilla bean

3 ripe mangoes, finely diced

¾ cup sugar

½ cup water

VANILLA GLAZE

2 cups icing sugar

3 tbsp milk (approx.)

½ tsp vanilla extract

One thing I like to do for birthday cakes is to individually tailor them to the person's favourite flavours. Folks who follow *RockRecipes.com* know how much Spouse loves her gingerbread and I had wanted to develop a quick, one bowl, simplified version of her favourite cake. It came together in no time—plus it turned out beautifully moist and well spiced.

To complement the cake, I filled it with some very easy to prepare vanilla mango jam and a simple vanilla glaze. Spouse loved it and so did the kids. We normally send out leftover dessert to friends and neighbors, but on this occasion, there was nothing but crumbs left on the plate by the next day.

GINGERBREAD CAKE

1. Preheat oven to 350°F.

2. Combine all ingredients in a mixing bowl and beat with electric mixer for 2-3 minutes.

3. Pour into 2 greased and floured 8- or 9-inch cake pans. Line the bottoms with parchment paper circles for easier release. Bake for 30-40 minutes or until a toothpick inserted in the center comes out clean. Cool in the pans for 10 minutes before turning out onto a wire rack to cool completely. Fill between the two layers with Mango Vanilla Jam.

MANGO VANILLA JAM

1. Split the vanilla bean lengthwise and scrape out the seed paste with a knife. Add the scraped out seeds, along with the vanilla pod, to a small saucepan along with the remaining ingredients. Bring to a very slow simmer for about 30 minutes or until almost all of the liquid has boiled off. Mash with a fork and set aside to cool completely before using to fill the cake.

VANILLA GLAZE

1. Mix all ingredients together until smooth. If it is too thick to flow properly, add a few more drops of milk, or if too thin, add a couple tablespoons icing sugar until you get the right consistency.

2. Spread the vanilla glaze over the top of the cake, letting it drizzle down the sides. Garnish with a dollop of the jam or fresh mango slices in the center of the cake.

Cherry Pecan Cake

PREP TIME: **30** MINUTES | COOK TIME: **60** MINUTES | SERVES **18** OR MORE

The more I think and write about old family recipes that have made appearances on *RockRecipes.com*, the more I begin to see them as connections to people and places. Some of them have a genealogy of sorts, and to trace the connections of who passed them on to friends and family would be a trip through time and through part of the food heritage of Newfoundland. This particular recipe has been in my family for about 30 years. I remember my mom getting this recipe from her twin sister, "Aunt Moo," who in turn got it from Ivy Loder of Badger, Newfoundland, a great family friend of many years to whom it had also been passed on.

I would hazard to say that this very moist, rich, and delicious cake has been made hundreds of times by people in my extended family. I make it at least a few times a year myself and have made it as a wedding cake for numerous friends and acquaintances over the years. Once you taste this cake, you can easily imagine just how many requests for the recipe come my way after it's served at a wedding reception. You're invited to join in the continuing legacy of one of the most delicious cakes I have ever eaten.

¾ cup **toasted pecan pieces** (not ground)

2 cups chopped (in halves or thirds) **maraschino cherries**

1½ cups **sugar**

1 cup **cream cheese** (8 oz)

1 cup **butter**

1½ tsp **pure vanilla extract**

4 **eggs**

2 + ¼ cups **flour**

1½ tsp **baking powder**

1. Preheat oven to 350°F. Toast the pecans on a cookie sheet for about 7 minutes in the oven. Let them cool then give them a rough chop with a sharp cook's knife.

2. Drain the cherries very well in a colander, tossing them for a couple of minutes to make sure any liquid trapped at the centers escapes. Drain well on paper towels for several minutes then chop the cherries as instructed and set aside.

3. Preheat oven to 325°F.

4. This cake can bake in a Bundt pan or in 2 regular loaf pans. If using a Bundt pan, grease it very well and lightly dust with flour. If using loaf pans, lightly grease them and line with parchment paper.

5. Cream together the sugar, cream cheese, butter, and vanilla extract for several minutes until light and fluffy. Scrape down the sides and bottom of the bowl a couple of times during this process.

6 Add the eggs one at a time, beating for a minute or so between additions.

7. Sift together 2 cups of the flour with the baking powder. Gently fold the dry ingredients into the creamed mixture until the flour is almost fully incorporated.

8. Toss the cherries in the ¼ cup of reserved flour and add them immediately to the batter along with the chopped pecans. Any flour that doesn't stick to the cherries gets added too. Fold until the flour is fully incorporated and the cherries and nuts are evenly dispersed throughout the batter.

9. Bake for about 1 hour or until a wooden toothpick inserted in the center of the cake comes out clean. The Bundt pan may take several minutes more; the loaf pans may need a little less, depending on your oven and the type of pans you're using. Always check your cakes a few minutes ahead of time and then every five minutes thereafter to make sure they do not over bake.

10. When fully baked, let the cakes rest in the pans for 10-15 minutes before turning out on a wire rack to cool completely.

Sticky Toffee Banana Cake
with Cream Cheese Frosting

PREP TIME: **45** MINUTES | COOK TIME: **30** MINUTES | SERVES **12–16**

STICKY TOFFEE BANANA CAKE

2¼ cups pureed **very ripe banana**

1 tsp **baking soda**

½ cup **butter**

1¼ cups firmly packed **brown sugar**

2 tsp **vanilla extract**

⅓ cup dark **corn syrup** (or golden syrup)

3 large **eggs**

2½ cups **all-purpose flour**

2 tsp **baking powder**

CREAM CHEESE FROSTING

1 cup **cream cheese**

½ cup **butter**

½ cup **shortening**

2 tbsp **vanilla extract**

1 kilo bag (about 8–9 cups) of **icing sugar** (powdered sugar)

1–3 tbsp **milk** (enough to bring the frosting to a spreadable consistency)

Hands up—who has brown speckled bananas on their countertop right now? Okay, put 'em down, that's all of you! They always seem to regenerate themselves on my countertop too. I hate wasting anything, so a good portion of my recipes get their inspiration just from the need to use up an ingredient rather than throw it out. Such was the case once with a small bunch of bananas that spent the better part of a week in their lonely, abandoned vigil on the counter. It was time to give them a purpose in life.

This cake does not have a typical cake-like texture. Like a good sticky toffee pudding, it collapses in your mouth to a dense, rich, caramel-like, luscious bite that is simply addictive. It's fantastic with the cream-cheese frosting as pictured, but if you're a fan of chocolate and banana flavours together, using a fudge-type frosting is amazingly delicious too.

STICKY TOFFEE BANANA CAKE

1. Preheat the oven to 350°F.

2. Grease and flour two 9-inch round cake pans and line the bottoms with parchment paper. The parchment paper greatly aids the release of the cakes from the pans when baked.

3. Mix together the pureed banana and baking soda and set aside.

4. Cream together the butter, brown sugar, and vanilla well.

5. Beat in the dark corn syrup (or golden syrup).

6. Beat in the eggs, one at a time, beating well after each addition.

7. Add the banana mixture and blend until smooth.

8. Sift together the flour and baking powder.

9. Add the dry ingredients to the creamed mixture in three equal portions mixing until smooth after each addition.

10. Pour into the prepared pans and bake for 30-35 minutes or until a toothpick inserted in the center comes out clean.

11. Let the cakes rest in the pans for 10-15 minutes before turning them out onto a wire rack to cool completely. Frost with Cream Cheese Frosting.

CREAM CHEESE FROSTING

1. Mix all the frosting ingredients together and beat well until smooth and fluffy. Add only a little milk at first and just add a little at a time until you get the perfect spreadable consistency.

2. If you don't plan on covering the cake completely in frosting, a half-batch of the recipe is plenty to fill the center and cover the top. With such a rich cake, you may want to serve it with less frosting, as I most often do.

The Ultimate Strawberries and Cream Cake

PREP TIME: **45** MINUTES | COOK TIME: **30** MINUTES | SERVES **10–12**

SHORTCUT SPONGE CAKE
6 **eggs**

1 cup **sugar**

3 tsp **vanilla extract**

1 cup **flour**

STRAWBERRY COMPOTE
4 cups **fresh** or **frozen strawberries**, cut in quarters

¾ cup **sugar**

2 rounded tbsp **cornstarch**

¼ cup **water**

VANILLA WHIPPED CREAME
2 cups **whipping cream**

4 tbsp **icing sugar** (powdered sugar)

2 tsp **vanilla extract**

1 lb of **fresh strawberries**, washed, hulled, and sliced

This beautiful cake just looks like summer, doesn't it? This is one of my recipes where, as sometimes happens, I decide not to decide. I knew I was using a shortcut sponge cake as the base, but this time the choice was whether to use fresh strawberries on the cake or to make a simple strawberry compote to layer with the cream. With two packages of strawberries on hand, I decided to use one fresh, turn the other into compote, and use both. The strawberry compote adds a little extra sweetness to the cake while the fresh strawberries offer bright fresh taste. It turned out to be a cake that actually does taste as good as it looks.

SHORTCUT SPONGE CAKE

1. Preheat oven to 350°F.

2. Line the bottoms of 2 ungreased 8-inch cake pans with parchment paper.

3. In the bowl of an electric mixer with the whisk attachment in place, add the eggs, sugar, and vanilla extract. Beat at high speed until the mixture is very light and foamy and about tripled in volume.

4. Remove the bowl from the mixture and very gently fold in the flour, a little at a time. I like to sprinkle the flour over the surface of the batter a little at a time and gently fold in with a rubber spatula.

5. Pour into the prepared pans and bake 25-30 minutes or until the cake springs back at the center and a wooden toothpick inserted in the center comes out clean.

6. Cool completely on a wire rack before splitting each layer with a serrated bread knife to create 4 layers in total.

STRAWBERRY COMPOTE

1. Wash and hull the strawberries and cut them into slices. Toss the strawberries in the sugar and let sit for 30 minutes. This will help to draw the juice from the strawberries before cooking them.

2. Bring the strawberries and sugar to a very gentle simmer for about 5-10 minutes.

3. Dissolve the cornstarch in the water and slowly add to the simmering strawberries as you stir gently but continuously. Bring the mixture back up to a gentle simmer and cook for an additional minute before removing from the heat and cooling completely. Chill in the fridge when it reaches room temperature.

VANILLA WHIPPED CREAM

1. Simply beat the whipping cream, icing sugar, and vanilla extract in the bowl of an electric mixer until firm peaks form.

to construct the cake >

Place the first layer on the cake plate and top with half the vanilla whipped cream and sliced berries. Add the next layer of cake and then half the strawberry sauce. Continue by adding the next layer of cake, whipped cream, and fresh strawberries. Add the final layer of cake and top with the remaining half of the strawberry sauce. Garnish with additional whipped cream and fresh strawberries if desired. Chill for a couple of hours before serving.

SPICE VELVET CAKE

1¼ cups sifted **all-purpose flour**

1½ cups sifted **cake flour**

½ tsp **baking soda**

1½ tsp **baking powder**

1 tsp **cinnamon**

½ tsp **ground ginger**

½ tsp **allspice**

¼ tsp **ground nutmeg**

¼ tsp **ground cloves**

1 tsp **salt**

1½ cups **sugar**

⅔ cup **vegetable oil**

⅓ cup **vegetable shortening** at room temperature

2 tsp **vanilla extract**

3 large **eggs**

1½ cups **buttermilk**

BROWN BUTTER FROSTING

1 cup **butter**, browned

4 cups **icing sugar** (powdered sugar)

2 tsp **vanilla extract**

3–4 tbsp **milk** (approx.)

Spice Velvet Cake

PREP TIME: 20 MINUTES | COOK TIME: 35 MINUTES
SERVES 12–16

This is a new addition to the now famous Velvet Cake Collection on *RockRecipes.com*. Other versions of this popular recipe have received hundreds of thousands of shares on social media over the last couple of years. The soft, moist crumb structure is what makes these recipes such successes. I've loved good spice cake since I was a kid, so developing this version was inevitable. With its caramel-flavoured brown butter frosting, it may just be my personal favourite yet. It's another one of those simple but delicious cakes that reminds me of Sunday dinner dessert as a kid.

SPICE VELVET CAKE

1. Preheat oven to 325°F.

2. Sift together both flours, baking soda, baking powder, cinnamon, ginger, allspice, nutmeg, cloves, salt, and sugar. Set aside.

3. Grease and flour two 9-inch round cake pans and line the bottom with 2 circles of parchment paper.

4. In the bowl of an electric mixer, beat together the vegetable oil, shortening, and vanilla. Beat well at high speed with whisk attachment until light and fluffy

5. Beat the eggs in one at a time.

6. Fold in the dry ingredients alternately with the buttermilk.

7. I always add dry ingredients in 3 divisions and liquid ingredients in 2 divisions. It is very important to begin and end the additions with the dry ingredients. Do not overmix the batter. As soon as it has no lumps in the batter, pour into the 2 prepared 9-inch cake pans.

8. Bake for 30-35 minutes or until a wooden toothpick inserted in the center comes out clean. Allow the cake to cool in the pans for 10 minutes before turning out onto wire racks to cool completely.

BROWN BUTTER FROSTING

1. To brown butter, just melt it in a small saucepan over medium heat and watch it carefully until the colour turns light golden brown. Watch it carefully; it can burn quickly once it reaches the proper colour.

2. Pour it off immediately into a heatproof measuring cup, leaving the sediment behind. Allow the brown butter to cool to room temperature and solidify.

3. Beat all ingredients together until smooth and fluffy with a spreadable consistency. Use a couple of tablespoons of milk to begin and add more if need be, or of it becomes too thin, just add a couple more tablespoons of icing sugar at a time to get to the proper consistency.

VANILLA CAKE

2¼ cups **all-purpose flour**

1¾ cups **cake flour**

4 tsp **baking powder**

¼ tsp **salt**

1½ cup **unsalted butter**, at room temperature

3 cups **sugar**

6 **eggs** at room temperature

2 tbsp **pure vanilla extract**

1½ cups **undiluted evaporated milk**

STRAWBERRY COMPOTE

4 cups **fresh** or **frozen strawberries**, cut in quarters

¾ cup **sugar**

2 rounded tbsp **cornstarch**

¼ cup **water**

VANILLA CUSTARD

3 cups **whole milk**

⅓ cup **flour**

⅔ cup **sugar**

pinch of **salt**

3 slightly beaten, **extra-large egg yolks**

4 tbsp **butter**

2 tbsp good quality **vanilla extract**

CHOCOLATE BUTTERCREAM FROSTING

2 cups **sugar**

⅔ cups **water**

6 **egg whites** at room temperature

¼ tsp **cream of tartar**

2 tsp **vanilla extract**

pinch of **salt**

2 cups **softened unsalted butter**

1 lb good quality **chocolate** (not milk chocolate), chopped in small pieces

½ cup **butter**

Too Tall Neapolitan Cake

PREP TIME: 90 MINUTES

COOK TIME: 35 MINUTES | SERVES **16** OR MORE

So you're probably already skimming through this long recipe and thinking, "Why did he include such an involved recipe in this cookbook?" The reason is simple. When I put together show-stopper desserts like this one, I don't think of them as a single recipe but more as a collection of individual recipes that make the whole. It's far less intimidating to approach it as four simpler recipes than as one that you perceive as complicated. When you break it down, it really isn't difficult.

And more than that, these four recipes will come in handy for other desserts you can create on your own. The yellow vanilla cake is a great stand-alone recipe for a large, three-layer cake to cover with any favourite frosting. The strawberry compote can top cheesecakes or sundaes. The vanilla custard makes a terrific filling for a vanilla cream pie or to layer into a delicious trifle. The Italian meringue-based chocolate buttercream frosting is the most involved of them all, I know, but once you master the skill of making this lusciously silky frosting, you will become famous for it! Put your imagination to work and dream up a new favourite dessert. The components of this amazing celebration cake hold loads of possibilities.

VANILLA CAKE

1. Preheat oven to 325°F. Grease and flour three 9-inch cake pans and line the bottoms with parchment paper.

2. Sift together the flour, cake flour, baking powder, and salt. Set aside.

3. Cream together the butter and sugar very well for several minutes. Scrape down the sides and bottom of the bowl a couple of times during this process.

4. Add the eggs, one at a time, beating for about 1 minute after each addition. Beat in the vanilla extract.

5. Gently fold in the dry ingredients in 3 equal portions alternately with the evaporated milk, which gets added in 2 equal portions so that you always start and end with dry ingredients.

6. Divide the batter evenly into the 3 prepared pans. Bake for about 35-40 minutes or until a toothpick inserted in the center comes out clean. Watch it carefully, you will not want to overbake this cake. As soon as the toothpick comes out clean, remove the cake from the oven and let it rest in the pans for 5 minutes before turning it out onto a wire rack to cool completely. When completely cool, split each layer horizontally to create 6 layers in total.

STRAWBERRY COMPOTE

1. Preheat oven to 325°F. Grease and flour three 9-inch cake pans and line the bottoms with parchment paper.

2. Bring the strawberries and sugar to a very gentle simmer for about 5-10 minutes.

3. Dissolve the cornstarch in the water and slowly add to the simmering strawberries as you stir gently but continuously. Bring the mixture back up to a gentle simmer and cook for an additional minute before removing from the heat and cooling completely. Chill in the fridge when the compote reaches room temperature.

VANILLA CUSTARD

1. Scald the milk almost to boiling point in the microwave.

2. In a medium-sized saucepan, combine the flour, sugar, and salt. Over medium heat, slowly add the scalded milk, whisking constantly. Continue to cook over medium heat until mixture begins to slightly thicken.

3. At this point, remove from heat and pour about ½ cup of this mixture onto the beaten egg yolks, whisking constantly. Pour the egg mixture immediately back into the pot with the rest of the custard, continuing to constantly stir. Cook for an additional minute or two until the custard reaches pudding consistency and remove from the flame.

4. Stir in the butter, 1 tbsp at a time, and finally the vanilla extract. Let the custard cool for 30 minutes, stirring occasionally, before moving it to the fridge to cool completely for a couple of hours.

CHOCOLATE BUTTERCREAM FROSTING

1. Combine the sugar and water and bring to a gentle boil. Continue to boil over medium heat without stirring until the mixture reaches 240°F on a candy thermometer.

2. Meanwhile, in the bowl of a large electric stand mixer, beat the egg whites, cream of tartar, vanilla extract, and salt together until stiff peaks form. When the sugar syrup has reached temperature, with the mixer running on medium, slowly pour in the sugar syrup in a thin stream hitting the side of the bowl and not the beaters. Be very careful as this syrup is very, very hot.

3. Continue beating the frosting for 15 minutes or longer until the meringue is completely cool. I hold ice wrapped in dishtowels around the bowl as it beats, to cool the meringue down more quickly.

4. While the meringue is cooling, melt the chocolate and the ½ cup of butter together in a double boiler, stirring often. Heat only enough to melt the chocolate, then remove from the heat. Set aside.

5. When the meringue in the mixer is completely cool to almost room temperature, slowly begin to add the butter, a few tablespoons at a time, without turning off the mixer.

6. Slowly mix in the melted chocolate and then continue to beat well at medium-high speed until frosting reaches a spreadable consistency. This may take 15 minutes or so and you may have to chill the frosting for several minutes before beating it again to get it to stiffen. Alternatively, you can place the frosting bowl in an ice bath while continuing to beat constantly with a hand-held until the icing stiffens sufficiently.

to assemble the cake

> Use a piping bag or a Ziploc bag with the corner snipped off to pipe a ½-inch wide line of frosting around the perimeter of the first layer of cake. This step is important for each layer because it will keep the fillings from spilling out as you assemble the cake. Fill the center of the ring with ⅓ of the vanilla custard and place another layer of cake on top. Again pipe another line of frosting around the perimeter of this layer and fill the center with strawberry compote. Continue alternating the layers until all six are used. Frost the entire outside of the cake with chocolate buttercream frosting. I recommend making this cake the day before serving and chilling it overnight in the fridge, so that it will stand up well and cut cleanly. Garnish with chocolate dipped strawberries if desired.

Brandied Peach Shortcake

PREP TIME: 35 MINUTES + SITTING TIME | **COOK TIME: 25** MINUTESS | SERVES **12**

Maybe it comes from a long-held love of a traditional sherry trifle, but I've always been partial to boozy desserts. Aromatic liquors or sweet, intensely flavoured liqueurs add a new dimension to many desserts and a real sense of celebration to any occasion. Summer peach season is one of my most anticipated points on the calendar, when those fantastic Ontario peaches I remember from childhood arrive in local markets. It's a time when peach pie and this shortcake always get made at our house.

This is still a great simple summer dessert for teetotalers if you want to leave out the brandy, especially if you have fresh, perfectly ripe, juicy peaches at the height of their seasonal perfection. Good quality canned or bottled peaches can be used off-season as a welcome reminder of summer.

VANILLA WHIPPED CREAM

2 cups **whipping cream**

2 tsp **vanilla extract**

4 rounded tbsp **icing sugar** (powdered sugar)

BRANDIED PEACH SHORTCAKE

10 **large fully ripe peaches**, peeled and sliced

4 oz **brandy** (rum or bourbon are also good)

¾ cups **sugar**

½ cup **cream cheese**

½ cup **butter**

1 tsp **vanilla extract**

2 **eggs**

1 cup **cake flour**

1 tsp **baking powder**

VANILLA WHIPPED CREAM

1. Beat the whipping cream, vanilla extract, and icing sugar together until firm peaks form.

BRANDIED PEACH SHORTCAKE

1. Toss the peach slices in the brandy, cover, and let sit for 1-2 hours before putting together the shortcake. Toss the peaches a couple of times during this time.

2. Preheat oven to 325°F.

3. To prepare the shortcake base, cream together the sugar, cream cheese, butter, and vanilla extract for several minutes until light and fluffy.

4. Add the eggs one at a time, beating well after each addition.

5. Sift together the cake flour and baking powder. Gently fold the dry ingredients into the creamed mixture.

6. Bake the base in a greased and parchment-lined 10- or 11-inch tart pan or springform pan for about 25 minutes or until a toothpick inserted in the center comes out clean. Cool on wire rack.

to construct the cake > Place the cooled shortcake base on a cake plate, drain the brandy off the peaches and sprinkle it over the surface of the cake. Arrange the peach slices in a circular pattern over the cake and top with the vanilla whipped cream.

Double Chocolate Truffle Cake

PREP TIME: 40 MINUTES **+ CHILLING TIME** | **COOK TIME: 35** MINUTESS | **SERVES 12–16**

This decadent cake would be the perfect centerpiece of any celebration dinner. A gorgeous chocolate cake always impresses, but just wait for the oohs and aahs when you cut into this cake to reveal the layers of velvety smooth white-chocolate truffle filling inside. It's definitely one to keep in mind to treat your favourite chocoholic on their next birthday.

CHOCOLATE SCRATCH CAKE

2 cups sugar

2 cups all-purpose flour

¾ cup cocoa

2 tsp baking powder

1 tsp baking soda

½ tsp salt

2 eggs

1 cup soured milk

1 cup black coffee

½ cup vegetable oil

1 tsp vanilla extract

WHITE CHOCOLATE TRUFFLE FILLING

2 cups white-chocolate chips

2 cups whipping cream

2 rounded tbsp icing sugar (powdered sugar)

1 tsp vanilla extract

CHOCOLATE TRUFFLE FROSTING

2 cups dark-chocolate chips

2 cups whipping cream

2 rounded tbsp icing sugar (powdered sugar)

1 tsp vanilla extract

CHOCOLATE SCRATCH CAKE

1. Preheat oven to 350°F.

2. Combine all the ingredients in a mixing bowl and beat with electric mixer for 2 minutes.

3. Pour into 2 greased and floured 9-inch cake pans.

4. Bake for 30-35 minutes or until a toothpick inserted in the center comes out clean. Cool in pans for 5 minutes before turning out onto a wire rack to cool completely.

5. When completely cooled, use a large serrated bread knife to cut the two cake layers into four.

WHITE CHOCOLATE TRUFFLE FILLING

1. In a double boiler, melt the white-chocolate chips together with ⅓ cup of the whipping cream. Stir constantly as you melt the chocolate and don't let it overheat. As soon as the last of the chocolate melts, take it immediately off the heat and let it cool down to lukewarm.

2. Whip the remaining 1⅔ cups cream with the icing sugar and vanilla to firm peaks and fold in the melted white chocolate by hand.

CHOCOLATE TRUFFLE FROSTING

1. Prepare the Chocolate Truffle Frosting using the same directions as the White Chocolate Truffle Filling.

to assemble the cake >

1. Use a piping bag or a Ziploc bag with the corner snipped off to pipe a ½-inch wide line of chocolate truffle frosting around the perimeter of the first layer of cake. This step is important for each layer because it will keep the filling from spilling out as you assemble the cake.

2. Fill the center of the ring with ⅓ of the white chocolate truffle filling and place another layer of cake on top. Continue for the next two layers, then place the final layer of cake on top.

3. Frost the sides and top of the cake with the chocolate truffle frosting. Garnish with grated chocolate or chocolate curls if you like.

4. Chill the cake very well for several hours or overnight before serving.

My favourite part about entertaining is coming up with a fantastic dessert to serve at the end of dinner. I'm still an unapologetic dessert junkie, but I'm also addicted to the reactions of like-minded dessert fanatics whose eyes bulge at the tempting creation being brought to the table. This collection of desserts includes recipes from some of my standard favourites, like Pecan Pie, to real showstoppers, like Carrot Cake Cheesecake. They are all sure to make you very popular with the dessert lovers in your life.

desserts

Perfect Cherry Cobbler 254

Mini Black Forest Cheesecakes 256

Perfect Pecan Pie 258

British Custard Tart 260

Mango Peach Coconut Crumble 262

Rum Raisin Ice Cream 264

Old-Fashioned Lemon Icebox Pie 266

Chocolate Cherry Upside-Down Cake 268

The Best Apple Pie (Noah's "Just an Apple Pie") 270

Carrot Cake Cheesecake 274

Frozen Peanut Butter Cup Pie 276

Blueberry Apple Upside-Down Cake 278

White Chocolate Cheesecake *with* Raspberries 280

Blueberry Fool Creampuffs 282

Perfect Cherry Cobbler

PREP TIME: **30** MINUTES | COOK TIME: **30** MINUTES | SERVES **6–8**

I love a great cherry cobbler, probably because I particularly love warm-from-the-oven, comfort-food desserts. I don't like the fruit to be cloyingly sweet though, as I've found in some restaurant versions. The cherries that I use are generally sweet enough anyway, and if yours are particularly naturally sweet, you can even cut the sugar used in the fruit layer by half.

A great cobbler is always amazing when you use fresh fruit, but when cherries are not in season, you can still make this delicious dessert using frozen cherries as in the version shown in the photograph. It makes a terrific Sunday dinner dessert, especially with a scoop of good vanilla ice cream.

FRUIT LAYER

4 cups fresh or frozen pitted cherries

½ cup sugar

1 tsp vanilla extract

¼ tsp cinnamon

1½ tsp cornstarch

¼ cup water

COBBLER DOUGH

1½ cups flour

½ cup sugar

1½ tsp baking powder

¼ cup + 2 tbsp very cold butter, cut in cubes

1 egg

½ cup milk

2 tsp vanilla extract

FRUIT LAYER

1. Bring the cherries, sugar, vanilla, and cinnamon to a slow simmer for about 5 minutes.

2. Dissolve the cornstarch in the water, and then stir this into the fruit mixture.

3. Pour the fruit into a 9x9-inch baking pan.

COBBLER DOUGH

1. Preheat oven to 350°F.

2. Sift together the flour, sugar, and baking powder.

3. Cut the butter in with a pastry blender or by pulsing it in a food processor until it resembles a coarse meal.

4. Separately beat together the egg, milk, and vanilla extract, and then add this to the dry ingredients and mix together just until a dough forms.

5. Drop the dough by heaping tablespoonfuls onto the hot cherries.

6. Bake for approximately 30 minutes or until the cherries are bubbling at the center of the pan and the top of the cobbler is golden brown.

Mini Black Forest Cheesecakes

PREP TIME: 30 MINUTES | **COOK TIME: 20** MINUTES | **MAKES 12** CUPCAKE-SIZED CHEESECAKES

CHOCOLATE COOKIE CRUST
¾ cup chocolate cookie crumbs

2½ tbsp melted butter

1 tbsp sugar

CHEESECAKE BATTER
1 cup cream cheese (one 8-oz block)

⅓ cup sugar

4 rounded tbsp cocoa powder

1½ tsp pure vanilla extract

1 egg

⅓ cup whipping cream

CHERRY COMPOTE
1½ cups fresh pitted cherries

¼ cup sugar

½ cup water (split into two ¼ cups)

1 rounded tsp cornstarch

VANILLA WHIPPED CREAM
¾ cup whipping cream

½ tsp vanilla extract

1½ tbsp icing sugar (powdered sugar)

3 tbsp grated chocolate for garnish

Eating well is not all about sacrifice. Indulgence is not a bad thing; in fact, I think it's good for the soul. It's always *overindulgence* that gets you into trouble. At only about 200 calories each, these beautifully enticing little Black Forest Cheesecakes are the perfect balance of portion control and luscious indulgence.

Let's face it, portion sizes of things like cheesecake, as served in restaurants, are massive by comparison and would likely come in at 3 or more times the number of calories in one of these cupcake-sized treats. I don't know that I have ever ordered a piece of cheesecake in a restaurant that Spouse and I haven't shared. I know oftentimes this is about presentation; restaurants do like to put out an impressive looking plate while encouraging the perception that more is good value. Realistically though, the vast majority of "sweet tooth" cravings will be completely satisfied by far less. That's why these are the perfect balance of maximum indulgence with minimum guilt.

CHOCOLATE COOKIE CRUST
1. Place paper liners in a 12-muffin pan.

2. In a bowl, mix together the cookie crumbs, butter, and sugar.

3. Divide evenly between the 12 paper-lined muffin cups and press the crumbs firmly into the bottom of each.

CHEESECAKE BATTER
1. Preheat oven to 300°F.

2. Mix together the cream cheese, sugar, cocoa, and vanilla until smooth.

3. Beat in the egg.

CHERRY COMPOTE

1. Add the cherries, sugar, and ¼ cup water to a small saucepan and very slowly bring it up to a simmer. You don't want to boil this mixture rapidly because you don't want to break the cherries down completely.

2. Simmer very slowly for only 3-4 minutes.

3. Dissolve the cornstarch in the remaining ¼ cup room-temperature water and then stir it slowly into the boiling mixture.

4. Bring it back up to a slow simmer and cook for only another 1-2 minutes until the compote thickens.

5. Remove from the heat and cool completely to room temperature.

4. Finally blend in the whipped cream until smooth.

5. Divide the cheesecake filling equally between the 12 muffin cups and bake for 15-20 minutes until the cheesecake has set and does not jiggle when you give the pan a slight shake.

6. Remove from the oven and cool completely.

VANILLA WHIPPED CREAM

1. Beat together the whipping cream, vanilla, and icing sugar to firm peaks. Transfer to a piping bag with a large star tip, or if you don't have a piping bag, just use a large Ziploc bag with a ½-inch opening snipped off the corner.

2. Pipe a ring of whipped cream around the outer edge of the cooled cheesecakes, spoon some cherry compote into the center of the ring, and garnish with a sprinkle of grated chocolate.

Perfect Pecan Pie

PREP TIME: **40** MINUTES | COOK TIME: **50** MINUTES | SERVES **12**

This is a pie I usually only make on special occasions. The reason is simple: There is a very real danger that I might eat the entire thing. Not all in a single go, mind you, but this is a recipe that I've been making for over 30 years and I absolutely, unabashedly love it. It is always on my Christmas dinner table every single year, and I sometimes request it for birthdays or Father's Day.

Although desserts are commonplace at my house, there are few that I am powerless to resist. But this is one of them. I find myself returning to the fridge time and time again to cut off "just a small sliver." Inside of two days, one Christmas, I basically ate close to an entire pie in small slivers! If you are a confirmed lover of pecan pie, this is your recipe. Even in my extensive travels throughout the southern US, I've never had better anywhere.

BUTTER PASTRY

1 cup **very cold butter**, cut in small cubes

2½ cups **flour**

2 tbsp **brown sugar**

½ tsp **salt**

1 tsp **vanilla extract**

¼-⅓ cup **ice water** + 2 tbsp **white vinegar** added (only enough liquid to make a dough form)

PECAN FILLING

4 large or extra-large **eggs**

1½ cups lightly packed **brown sugar**

1½ cups **dark corn syrup**

2 tsp **vanilla extract**

½ cup **melted butter**

1½ cups **pecan halves**

BUTTER PASTRY

1. Using a food processor or a pastry blender, cut the cold butter into the flour, brown sugar, and salt until the mixture resembles a coarse meal. Small pieces of butter should still be visible.

2. Pour vanilla into the ice water and vinegar mixture and then pour this over the butter mixture and work in by tossing with a fork until a dough begins to form. Use your hands as little as possible and work the dough as little as possible.

3. Divide dough into 2 balls, flatten into 2 rounds, wrap in plastic wrap and place in the refrigerator to rest for a minimum of 20 minutes. You can make your dough the previous day, but make sure you take it out of the fridge for 10 minutes to warm slightly before rolling out. (This pastry recipe can make two pie crusts, so wrap one of the pastry rounds tightly in aluminum foil and freeze it for later).

4. Roll the dough into a 12- to 14-inch round and place in the bottom of a 10-inch pie plate.

5. Push the dough into the corners and ensure that it is not stretched at all or it will shrink from the edge.

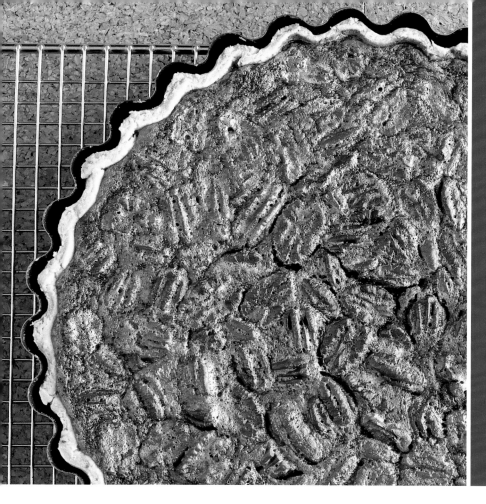

tip > The amount of egg used in this recipe is important. I generally use extra-large eggs, but if you have large, it shouldn't hurt to add an additional egg. And all corn syrup is not the same. Here it is very thick: thicker than molasses at room temperature. If your corn syrup isn't that thick, be sure to add that extra egg as insurance that the pie will set. Make sure you are using a large enough pie plate as well, or the filling will be too thick—a shallower pie is better for setting. I bake it in a 10-inch pie plate or even an 11-inch tart pan. As long as the crust doesn't burn, an extra few minutes in the oven should not be a problem if needed as well.

6. Trim dough to a ½-inch past the edge of the plate.

7. Fold the ends under and pinch with fingers or a fork to shape the edges into whatever design you like best.

8. Place in freezer while you prepare the filling.

PECAN FILLING

1. Preheat oven to 375°F.

2. Whisk the eggs, brown sugar, corn syrup, vanilla, and melted butter together until the brown sugar is dissolved.

3. Stir in the pecans.

4. Bake for 50-60 minutes or until the center is set and jiggles like jelly. Cool completely before serving.

PASTRY

1 cup **butter** (very cold and cut in small cubes)

2¼ cups flour

1 tbsp brown sugar

½ tsp **salt**

4–6 tbsp ice water

1 tsp white vinegar

BRITISH CUSTARD TART FILLING

2 cups whipping cream

1 cup whole milk

pinch **salt**

¼ tsp freshly ground nutmeg

the seed paste scraped from the inside of a small vanilla bean + the remaining vanilla pod

4 eggs

¾ cup light brown sugar, lightly packed

freshly grated nutmeg

British Custard Tart

PREP TIME: 30 MINUTES

COOK TIME: 1 HOUR 40 MINUTES | SERVES 8–10

I've seen this custard tart on many food shows from the UK. I love British cooking shows, and none more than the baking shows, which have always been my favourite, probably because I've been baking from a very early age. I have made a few versions of baked custard tarts and pies over the years, including one that seems to have become famous: my very easy Sour Cream Flan from the original *Rock Recipes* cookbook.

To me, this recipe does have a bit of a Christmas vibe because—with all the cream, eggs, and nutmeg included—it's very reminiscent of eggnog. I think it would make an ideal holiday celebration dessert.

> note > This pastry recipe is sufficient for 2 pie shells, but the second half of the pastry is easily formed into a flat round, wrapped tightly in a couple of layers of plastic wrap, and frozen for several weeks until you need it.

PASTRY

1. Pulse the cold butter into the flour, sugar, and salt using a food processor or pastry cutter until the butter is reduced to pea-sized pieces.

2. Remove to a large bowl. Combine the water and vinegar, sprinkle over the surface of the flour mixture, and toss with a fork until the water is just incorporated into the dough. Do not overwork the dough; handle it only enough so that the dough stays together.

3. Separate the dough into 2 balls and wrap in plastic. Place in the fridge to chill well. You can freeze one for another time.

4. Roll out into a 12-inch round and place into a 9-inch deep-dish pie plate or tart pan, being careful not to stretch the dough or it will shrink during baking. Trim the excess pastry from the edges and chill the pan for 10 minutes.

5. Preheat oven to 375°F.

6. Lay a sheet of parchment paper or aluminum foil over the pastry in the pan and fill the pan with baking weights. If you don't have baking weights, dry kidney beans or rice will do in a pinch; anything that will weigh down the bottom pastry so that it doesn't puff up. You can reuse dry beans many times for blind baking, so be sure to save them for that purpose.

7. Blind bake the pastry using the baking weights for about 15 minutes, remove the baking weights and parchment paper, and bake for another 10-15 minutes to crisp the bottom of the pie shell. Remove from the oven while you prepare the filling.

BRITISH CUSTARD TART FILLING

1. Reduce oven temperature to 300°F.

2. In a small saucepan over low heat, add the whipping cream, milk, salt, and vanilla pod. You want to heat this very slowly to almost boiling so the full flavour of the vanilla bean gets infused into the cream and milk. When heated, remove the vanilla bean and set aside for a couple of minutes. (In a pinch, 4 tsp of pure vanilla extract can be substituted for the vanilla bean.)

3. Whip together the eggs and brown sugar very well. Slowly whisk in the hot milk a little at a time; too fast and you'll scramble the eggs.

4. Remove from heat and pass the cream and egg mixture through a sieve into a large heatproof measuring cup or jug.

5. Place the blind-baked pie shell in its pan on a baking sheet. Pour in the cream and egg mixture until it has almost reached the top of the shell. Finely grate or sprinkle on a dusting of freshly grated nutmeg.

6. Place the baking sheet in the oven. If you have a little more cream mixture to bring the level to the top of the crust, you can carefully pour that into the pan when it is in the oven to avoid spillage. It's perfectly okay if you have a little of the filling mixture left over, pan sizes do vary.

7. Bake for 60-70 minutes. The top should be pale golden brown and the center will still jiggle a little.

8. Remove from the oven and let cool to almost room temperature before transferring to the fridge to cool and set completely. This will take several hours or overnight. Serve with fresh berries or seasonal fruit salad.

Mango Peach Coconut Crumble

PREP TIME: **20** MINUTES | COOK TIME: **50** MINUTES | SERVES **8–10**

All year I long for summer peaches. Peach season is always my favourite time in summer. I seem to spend those weeks every year making peach pies, cobblers, and crumbles like this one. My intention with this recipe was to add a taste of the tropics to my peach crumble by adding some sweet ripe mango. Those flavours go really well together. To add a further tropical touch, I included some dried coconut, but if you're not partial to coconut, you can just substitute oatmeal instead. In the winter, I make this with frozen peaches for another welcome taste of summer when it's most needed. It's wonderful with some good vanilla bean or coconut ice cream too.

FRUIT LAYER

3 large peaches, diced

2 small mangoes, diced

½ cup sugar

1½ tbsp cornstarch

pinch cinnamon

pinch salt

1½ tsp pure vanilla extract

2 tbsp lemon juice

COCONUT CRUMBLE TOPPING

1½ tsp baking powder

1¼ cups unsweetened dried coconut

1½ cups flour

¾ cup brown sugar

1 cup butter, cut in small cubes

FRUIT LAYER

1. You will need about 5-6 cups of fruit in total between the mango and peaches.

2. Mix together the sugar, cornstarch, cinnamon, and salt.

3. Toss together with the fruit mixture.

4. Mix in the vanilla and lemon juice.

5. Mix together well and pour fruit mixture evenly into the bottom of a 9x9- or 8x12-inch glass baking dish. A 10-inch deep-dish pie plate works well too.

COCONUT CRUMBLE TOPPING

1. Preheat oven to 350°F.

2. In a large bowl, toss together the baking powder, coconut, flour, and brown sugar.

3. Using your fingers, rub the butter thoroughly through the dry ingredients.

4. When the butter has been fully incorporated, you should be able to press the mixture together in your hands and it should hold together.

5. Break off small chunks and scatter them evenly over the surface of the prepared fruit. Press down lightly.

6. Bake for 40-50 minutes. The fruit should be bubbling and the crumble should be evenly golden brown when it is fully baked.

7. Allow to cool for at least 20 minutes before serving.

Rum Raisin Ice Cream

PREP TIME: **30** MINUTES **+** SOAKING TIME AND CHILLING TIME

COOK TIME: **5** MINUTES | MAKES ABOUT **1** QUART (**2** PINTS)

1 cup raisins

4 oz dark or amber rum
(dark rum has a deeper flavour
and adds colour)

2 cups whole milk

2 cups whipping cream
(35% milk fat)

6 egg yolks

1 cup sugar

1 tbsp pure vanilla extract

This recipe was absolutely developed with Spouse in mind. She is the ultimate fan of rum and raisin ice cream, and when her favourite premium brand stopped being carried in the super-markets here, I had to take up the torch and come up with a solution. Soaking the raisins in the rum for a full day is essential for this recipe and well worth the rewards of waiting. Spouse says it's the best she has ever tasted, even beating those famous premium brands in your supermarket freezer. If you are a fan of rum raisin ice cream, this homemade version may well be the best you will ever try.

1. Soak raisins in the rum overnight in an airtight container. I like to use a Mason jar so I can shake it every now and then to ensure the raisins are evenly soaked.

2. Combine the milk and cream and heat in the microwave (or on top of the stove over medium heat) to scalding but not boiling.

3. In a medium-sized saucepan, whisk together the egg yolks and sugar very well for about 3 minutes until the mixture is pale and fluffy.

4. Whisking constantly, add about a cup of the scalded milk to the egg yolk mixture. This tempers the egg yolks so they do not cook and scramble. Whisk in about another cup and make sure it is well blended with the egg yolk mixture. Finally, add the remaining scalded milk and cream and make sure it is well blended in.

5. Place the saucepan over medium heat and stir constantly but slowly for about 5 minutes until the mixture slightly thickens. At this point, you should be able to dip a wooden spoon in the custard and draw a distinct line with your finger on the back of the wooden spoon. Do not boil or the mixture may curdle.

6. Chill the custard very well for several hours or overnight. I chill it overnight while the raisins soak in the rum.

7. When completely chilled, stir the custard well and pour into your ice-cream maker. Process for 20-30 minutes until the ice cream becomes as thick as possible.

8. Transfer the ice cream quickly to a chilled metal or glass bowl and very quickly fold in the soaked raisins and any rum that has not been absorbed by them.

9. Place in an airtight container and freeze in the coldest part of your refrigerator freezer, or deep freezer, for several hours or preferably overnight before serving.

10. I like to fold the ice cream at least a couple of times every couple of hours to make sure all of the raisins do not settle to the bottom of the container and to make sure they get evenly distributed throughout the ice cream.

Old-Fashioned Lemon Icebox Pie

PREP TIME: **30** MINUTES + FREEZING TIME | COOK TIME: **15** MINUTES | SERVES **8**

This is by no means an original recipe but one that deserves a new lease on life. There are many slight variations of this recipe written everywhere from webpages to the side of condensed-milk cans. My version adds some finely minced lemon zest to give it a more intense, tangy lemon flavour, but it's still the same basic recipe that your grandmother may have made. Many recipes now use a graham-crumb crust, but the recipe I've used for years called for a vanilla-cookie-crumb crust, which is what I've used here along with additional wafer cookies for decoration like I once saw in an old cookbook. The filling freezes to a silky, luscious, creamy texture with plenty of lemony tart flavour. It's the ideal make-ahead dessert for Sunday dinner or a summer barbecue. Sometimes the oldest recipes really are the best.

3 cups **vanilla cookie crumbs** (I use Nilla cookies)

¾ cup **melted butter**

1 cup **whipping cream**

2 rounded tsp **icing sugar** (powdered sugar)

1 tsp **vanilla extract**

9 **extra-large egg yolks**

⅓ cup **sugar**

two 10-oz cans of **sweetened condensed milk**

1 cup **lemon juice**

zest of 2 lemons, finely minced (more or less to taste)

1. Preheat oven to 325°F.

2. Grease a 10-inch deep-dish pie plate or line the bottom of a 10-inch springform pan and lightly grease the sides.

3. Mix together the cookie crumbs and butter.

4. Press into the bottom and sides of the pie plate or to about ¾ of the height of a springform pan if you're using one.

5. Bake for 10 minutes, and then set aside to cool.

6. Whip the cream, icing sugar, and vanilla to soft peaks and set aside.

7. In the bowl of a stand mixer with the whisk attachment in place, add the egg yolks and ⅓ cup sugar.

8. Whisk at high speed until light, foamy, and pale yellow in colour (about 5 minutes).

9. Slowly whisk in the sweetened condensed milk, lemon juice, and zest (save some zest for garnish).

10. Gently fold in the previously whipped cream.

11. Pour into the prepared pie crust.

12. Freeze overnight.

13. Garnish with whipped cream, additional Nilla cookies, and lemon zest before serving.

Chocolate Cherry Upside-Down Cake

PREP TIME: **15** MINUTES | COOK TIME: **35** MINUTES | SERVES **8**

This quick and easy to prepare smaller-sized cake is an example of what I call a weeknight dessert. It really is very fast to put together and takes little more than 30 minutes in the oven, so you can slide it in next to those baked chicken breasts you're having for dinner. The reward is much greater than the effort in this case, and it's a surefire way to beat the mid-week blues. Start a "Hump Day" dessert night and see how much easier it will be to get through the week.

CHERRY LAYER

⅓ cup sugar

1 tsp cornstarch

2 cups fresh or frozen pitted cherries

CHOCOLATE CAKE BATTER

1 cup sugar

1 cup all-purpose flour

⅓ cup + 1 tbsp cocoa

1 tsp baking powder

½ tsp baking soda

¼ tsp salt

2 eggs

½ cup soured milk

½ cup black coffee

¼ cup vegetable oil

½ tsp vanilla extract

CHERRY LAYER

1. Grease and flour a 9-inch round pan that's at least 2 inches deep, and line the bottom with a round of parchment paper. You can also use an 8x8-inch square baking dish for this cake.

2. Blend together the sugar and cornstarch, and then toss the mixture well with the pitted cherries. If using frozen cherries, allow them to thaw for 20 minutes or so before using them.

3. Spread the cherries evenly over the bottom of the prepared pan.

CHOCOLATE CAKE BATTER

1. Preheat oven to 350°F.

2. Combine all ingredients in the batter recipe in a mixing bowl and beat with an electric mixer for 2 minutes.

3. Pour slowly and evenly over the cherries in the prepared cake pan.

4. Bake for 30-35 minutes or until a toothpick inserted in the center comes out clean. Cool in pans for 5 minutes before turning out onto a heatproof serving plate.

5. Serve warm or cold with ice cream or a dollop of freshly whipped cream.

The Best Apple Pie
(Noah's "Just an Apple Pie")

PREP TIME: 50 MINUTES + COOLING TIME | COOK TIME: 50 MINUTES | SERVES 8–10

PASTRY

½ cup **very cold butter**, cut in small cubes

½ cup **very cold vegetable shortening**, cut in small cubes

2½ cups **pastry flour** (preferable, but all-purpose can be used)

2 tbsp **brown sugar**

½ tsp **salt**

1 tbsp **plain white vinegar**

1 tsp **vanilla extract**

⅓ cup **ice water** (use only enough to make a dough form)

APPLE PIE FILLING

¼ cup **butter**

3 lb **Granny Smith apples**, peeled cored and sliced into thick wedges

2 cups **apple juice**

½ cup **brown sugar**

½ cup **white sugar**

1 tsp **ground cinnamon**

½ tsp **freshly ground nutmeg**

3 tbsp **cornstarch**

¼ cup **cold water**

1 large **egg yolk**

1–2 tbsp **water**

1–2 tbsp **turbinado sugar** (optional)

There is a bit of a secret technique in this recipe, but as my 13-year-old son reminded me the first time I made it, the best apple pie is still "just an apple pie." When I said I was making an apple pie, Noah perked up and inquired, "Just an apple pie?" When asked what he meant, he reiterated, "Just an apple pie; no exotic berries added, no fancy spices, no crumb topping...*just an apple pie*!?" What can I say? The boy is a purist.

The lesson, to be sure, is that some things need not be complicated. There's nothing wrong (and everything right) about "just" an apple pie, so that's what I made, but with a little twist that wouldn't offend his purist sensibilities. The technique of making the filling separately with the addition of reduced apple juice and then letting it cool before filling the pastry results in the most intensely flavoured apple pie you may ever eat. *Rock Recipes* fans who have made this recipe agree that it's the best.

PASTRY

1. Using a food processor or a pastry cutter, cut cold butter and shortening into the flour, brown sugar, and salt until mixture resembles a coarse meal. Small pieces of butter should still be visible.

2. Pour vinegar and vanilla into the ice water and then pour over the flour mixture and work in by tossing with a fork until a dough begins to form. Use your hands as little as possible and work the dough as little as possible.

3. Divide the dough into 2 balls, flatten into 2 rounds, wrap in plastic wrap, and place in the refrigerator to rest for a minimum of 20 minutes. You can make your dough the previous day, but make sure you take it out of the fridge for 10 minutes to warm slightly before rolling out.

APPLE PIE FILLING

1. Melt butter in a large non-stick pan over medium heat, and then add the apples and sauté for about 5 minutes until they are fully warmed throughout but not falling apart. Set aside to cool for a few minutes.

2. Meanwhile, simmer the apple juice over medium-low heat. Continue to simmer until the volume of juice has reduced to 1 cup.

3. Add the reduced juice to the apples and return to the stovetop on medium heat to get the mixture boiling, and then add the sugars, cinnamon, and nutmeg.

4. Simmer for only a minute before adding a thickening slurry made from dissolving together the cornstarch and ¼ cup of water.

5. Stir continuously as you add the cornstarch slurry and continue to simmer, stirring constantly for about a minute. Remove from heat and allow to cool to room temperature before using to fill the bottom pie crust.

6. Roll the first dough round into a 12-inch round and place in the bottom of a 10-inch pie plate. Push the dough into the corners and ensure that it is not stretched at all or it will shrink from the edge.

7. Trim dough to edge of plate. Add the cooled apple-pie filling.

tip > If your lattice crust edges begin to get too brown, just wrap them with aluminum foil for the last of the baking time.

8. Roll the remaining dough round into a 12-inch square-ish shape and cut that into 8 or 10 equal strips for the lattice crust top.

9. Place the remaining pastry strips on top of the apple-pie filling, interweaving them to form a simple lattice pattern.

10. Press the ends of the strips into the edge of the bottom crust and trim the excess with a sharp knife.

11. Brush the edges of the crust and the lattice top with an egg wash made by whisking together the egg yolk and water.

12. Sprinkle the lattice top with turbinado sugar if desired.

13. Chill the pie in the fridge for about 20-30 minutes before placing it on a cookie sheet (to catch any drips from the filling).

14. Preheat oven to 400°F.

15. Bake for 20 minutes (bottom rack is best) then reduce heat to 350°F and bake for an additional 30-35 minutes or until the crust is an even golden brown. The filling need not bubble for this pie to be done.

16. Allow to cool on a wire rack at room temperature for at least a couple of hours before serving.

Carrot Cake Cheesecake

PREP TIME: 30 MINUTES | **COOK TIME: 75** MINUTES | SERVES **12–16**

CARROT CAKE LAYER

1⅔ cups flour

¾ tsp baking powder

¾ tsp baking soda

1½ tsp cinnamon

½ tsp freshly grated nutmeg

½ tsp salt

1 cup sugar

2 eggs lightly beaten

⅔ cup vegetable oil

1 cup grated carrots

1 cup well-drained crushed pineapple

⅓ cup chopped pecans (optional)

CHEESECAKE LAYER

two 8-oz packages of cream cheese

⅔ cup sugar

2 eggs

2 tsp vanilla extract

⅓ cup whipping cream

Admittedly this recipe was inspired by a restaurant version that I'd seen online quite a few years ago. Theirs had cake batter swirled through the cheesecake batter, which I was quite skeptical about. I decided instead to see what would happen if I gently spooned my standard cheesecake batter over my standard carrot cake recipe in a layered fashion instead. It worked perfectly!

It's almost as if the carrot cake is frosted with a layer of cheesecake. When you think about it, we always have cream cheese frosting on carrot cake, so the combination of cheesecake and carrot cake is a natural. If you like carrot cake and *love* cheesecake, you'll find this recipe simply irresistible!

CARROT CAKE LAYER

1.   Grease and flour the bottom of a 10-inch springform pan. Do not grease the sides. Line the bottom with parchment paper.

2.   Sift together flour, baking powder, baking soda, cinnamon, nutmeg, and salt. Set these dry ingredients aside.

3.   In a large mixing bowl, beat the sugar, eggs, and oil until light and fluffy.

4.   Stir in the grated carrots, pineapple, and nuts.

5.   Fold in the dry ingredients by hand. Stir only until the dry ingredients are incorporated into the batter. Do not overmix.

6.   Pour evenly into prepared springform pan.

CHEESECAKE LAYER

1.   Preheat oven to 325°F.

2.   Cream together the cream cheese and sugar. Add the eggs, one at a time, beating well after each addition. Blend in the vanilla extract and whipping cream.

3. Spoon this cheesecake batter slowly and evenly over the carrot-cake batter already in the springform pan.

4. Bake for 30 minutes and then reduce the heat to 300°F and bake for an additional 45 minutes. A good time to take the cheesecake out of the oven is when it begins to turn brown at the edges. Cool on a wire rack for 15 minutes before running a sharp knife all the way around the inside edge of the cake. Leave on the wire rack until completely cooled, then refrigerate, remove from pan, and garnish with whipped cream and, if desired, candied carrot sticks.

to make candied carrot sticks > Cut a large peeled carrot into 2-inch sticks about a ¼-inch thick. Simmer in ½ cup water and ½ cup sugar until the carrots are cooked and the sugar solution is syrupy. Cool completely before using as a garnish.

Frozen Peanut Butter Cup Pie

PREP TIME: **30** MINUTES | FREEZING TIME: **6** HOURS | SERVES **12–16**

CHOCOLATE COOKIE CRUST
2⅔ cups chocolate cookie crumbs

⅔ cup melted butter

3 rounded tbsp white sugar

PEANUT BUTTER ICE CREAM FILLING
1 cup whipping cream

2 tbsp icing sugar (powdered sugar)

1 tsp vanilla extract

one 10-oz can of sweetened condensed milk

1 cup mascarpone cheese

¾ cup peanut butter

CHOCOLATE GANACHE TOPPING
2 cups semisweet chocolate chips

⅔ cup whipping cream, heated in the microwave to almost boiling

This pie has been one of the most popular dessert recipes from my blog on social media sites like Pinterest and Facebook over the last couple of years. Which is surprising because when you Google "peanut butter pie" you'll find more recipes than you can count.

I set out to develop my own recipe, and from the first bite I knew I had a winner. The creamy, no churn peanut butter ice-cream center is incredibly silky, as is the soft melt-in-your-mouth ganache top, with the crust adding a great textural crunch. Incredible! The recipe gets rave reviews from those who've tried it, and people love that it can be made a week or more in advance if needed. Peanut butter cup lovers in particular go wild for this pie.

CHOCOLATE COOKIE CRUST

1. Lightly grease the bottom and sides of a 9-inch springform pan. Line with parchment paper and then very lightly grease the parchment paper as well.

2. Mix together the crumbs, butter, and sugar.

3. Press the crumbs into the bottom and ¾ of the way up the sides of the prepared pan. Set aside.

PEANUT BUTTER ICE CREAM FILLING

1. Whip the whipping cream, icing sugar, and vanilla extract to firm peaks.

2. Slowly beat in the condensed milk.

3. Next, beat in the mascarpone cheese and peanut butter.

4. Pour into the prepared crust and freeze for several hours or preferably overnight.

CHOCOLATE GANACHE TOPPING

1. Melt together the chocolate chips and scalded whipping cream in a double boiler.

2. Reserve a little of the chocolate mixture to drizzle over the whipped cream if you like, then spread the rest over the top of the frozen pie.

3. Return to the freezer until ready to serve. Before serving you can garnish with whipped cream and a drizzle of the chocolate ganache as well as some roasted peanuts.

Blueberry Apple Upside-Down Cake

PREP TIME: **20** MINUTES | COOK TIME: **45** MINUTES | SERVES **9–12**

BLUEBERRY AND APPLE TOPPING
¼ cup melted butter

½ cup brown sugar

1 tsp cinnamon

½ tsp nutmeg

4 medium-sized apples, peeled, cored and sliced

¾ cup blueberries

CAKE BATTER
½ cup butter

½ cup sugar

2 eggs

2 tsp vanilla extract

2 cups flour

2 tsp baking powder

1 cup soured milk

This version of upside-down cake was inspired by an apple and blueberry pie I had in a diner in Vermont many years ago. I'd never had the combination before, and I thought they complimented each other beautifully. Back home, I eventually used the combination in an upside-down cake destined to become a family favourite.

This is the kind of dessert I would serve if we had weekday guests over for dinner. Working together, Spouse and I can have this in the oven in 20 minutes or less, and with a bake time of about 45 minutes, it's easy to serve this warm from the oven to an appreciative table. Apples are always plentiful, as are wild Newfoundland blueberries in our freezer courtesy of my berry-picking dad, so this is a particularly loved winter dessert in our family.

BLUEBERRY AND APPLE TOPPING
1. Preheat oven to 350°F.

2. In the bottom of a 9-inch square baking dish, combine the melted butter, brown sugar, cinnamon, and nutmeg.

3. Stir until well combined, and spread evenly in the bottom of the pan. Arrange the apples in a single layer on the top of the cinnamon and sugar mixture.

4. Sprinkle the blueberries evenly over the apples.

CAKE BATTER
1. Cream together the butter and sugar well.

2. Add the eggs, one at a time, beating well after each addition.

3. Beat in the vanilla extract.

4. Sift together the flour and baking powder.

5. Add dry ingredients to the creamed mixture alternately with the soured milk, beginning and ending with the dry ingredients.

6. Pour cake batter evenly over the prepared fruits and bake for 45-60 minutes or until toothpick inserted in center of the cake comes out clean.

7. Serve warm with ice cream or vanilla flavoured whipped cream.

GRAHAM CRUMB CRUST

1⅓ cups graham wafer crumbs

3 tbsp sugar

⅓ cup melted butter

WHITE CHOCOLATE CHEESECAKE WITH RASPBERRIES

⅓ cup whipping cream

1 cup good quality white-chocolate chips

three 8-oz packages of cream cheese

½ cup sugar

3 eggs

3 tsp vanilla extract

1 cup whipping cream

3–4 cups fresh raspberries

½ cup white-chocolate chips, melted (for garnish, optional)

White Chocolate Cheesecake *with* Raspberries

PREP TIME: **20** MINUTES | COOK TIME: **70** MINUTES
SERVES **16**

This is probably the cheesecake that I take along most often when bringing dessert to a potluck or other gathering. The combination of the delicate white-chocolate flavour and bright zing of fresh raspberries is always a real crowd pleaser and seems to be universally enjoyed by all, even those with fussy flavour preferences.

Cheesecake does not need to be heavy and stodgy. This recipe shows how to make it creamy and lusciously light textured. Totally uncomplicated but totally delicious, this one is in my personal top 5 favourite cheesecake recipes to ever appear on *RockRecipes.com* over the years. You just can't go wrong with something so simple yet so appealing.

GRAHAM CRUMB CRUST

1. In a small bowl, combine the graham crumbs, sugar, and melted butter.

2. Press into the bottom of a lightly greased 9- or 10-inch springform pan. (Grease the bottom only. I also like to line the bottom with parchment paper for easy release of the cheesecake from the pan when it has cooled.)

WHITE CHOCOLATE CHEESECAKE WITH RASPBERRIES

1. Preheat oven to 325°F.

2. In a double boiler, melt together the ⅓ cup whipping cream and 1 cup of white-chocolate chips. You want this just at the melting point, so be careful not to overheat it. Let it cool to lukewarm if necessary after melting. Set aside to cool while you prepare the rest of the cheesecake batter.

3. Cream together the cream cheese and ½ cup sugar for a few minutes, scraping the bowl often.

4. Add the eggs, one at a time, beating well after each addition.

5. Stir in the vanilla extract and melted white chocolate.

6. Finally blend in the 1 cup of whipping cream until smooth.

notes > A bain marie is simply a water bath that buffers the direct heat from the sides and bottom of the baking pan to more evenly bake the cheesecake.

I bake my cheesecakes in a 9- or 10-inch springform pan that has the bottom and sides wrapped in multiple layers of wide heavy-duty aluminum foil. This forms a sort of boat that the cheesecake pan sits in. The roll of aluminum foil I use is about 16 inches wide. I use at least 4 layers of foil to make sure that no water leaks in and ruins the crust of my cheesecake. As an extra precaution, there is no harm in wrapping the bottom of the pan in plastic wrap before adding the aluminum foil. The heat is not high enough to melt it and it doesn't come into contact with the cheesecake anyway. The aluminum foil wrapped pan is then placed inside a larger baking pan; I use a 12-inch cake pan. Boiling water is then poured into the larger pan filling it from ½ to ⅔ of the way to the top.

I find it best to pour the boiling water into the pan after it is placed on the rack in the oven as you are less likely to splash water onto the cheesecake or inside the aluminum foil. I reuse the aluminum foil for several future cheesecakes, adding a couple of layers to it each time just to be safe.

7. Pour over the prepared base and bake in a bain marie (see notes) for 60-70 minutes. The cheesecake may begin to lightly brown at the edges, but a cheesecake does not need to brown at all to be fully baked. The surface of the cheesecake should lose any shine when the cake is properly baked. It can still be slightly wobbly just at the center at this point.

8. Remove the cake from the oven and run a sharp knife completely around the edge of the pan. This will allow the cheesecake to shrink as it cools and hopefully not crack (but who cares if it does? I am never bothered by a crack or two in the surface).

9. Allow the cheesecake to cool thoroughly on a wire rack at room temperature. (Do not put a hot cheesecake into the fridge to cool quickly, this may result in an under-baked cheesecake because the residual heat actually continues to set the cheesecake after it comes out of the oven.)

10. When completely cool cover the top with fresh raspberries and garnish with melted white chocolate if desired.

11. Chill completely in the refrigerator until ready to serve.

Blueberry Fool Creampuffs

PREP TIME: **40** MINUTES | COOK TIME: **40** MINUTES | MAKES **18**

Choux pastry is what's used to make those light, airy pastry shells for creampuffs and éclairs. Many people are needlessly intimidated by its preparation when there's really no need to be. It's actually quite simple; in fact, I've been successfully making these since I was about 12. The biggest issue is under-baking, which causes them to collapse, but once you get the timing right, they're a breeze. Here I've filled them with a whipped cream and blueberry jam "fool" as an alternative to plain cream, but you can use any jam you like to create your own favourite version.

CHOUX PASTRY SHELLS

1 cup water

½ cup butter

1 cup all-purpose flour

¼ tsp salt

4 large or extra-large eggs

BLUEBERRY FOOL FILLING

3 cups whipping cream

3 rounded tbsp icing sugar (powdered sugar)

2 tsp vanilla extract

½ cup good quality blueberry jam

CHOUX PASTRY SHELLS

1. Add the water and butter to a medium-sized saucepan and bring to a gentle boil.

2. Reduce the heat to medium and quickly add the flour and salt all at once, stirring them in quickly to form a soft dough.

3. Cook this mixture, stirring constantly, for an additional 3 minutes.

4 Allow this mixture to cool slightly for about 10-15 minutes before adding the eggs, one at a time, stirring until smooth after each addition.

5. Cover and chill in the refrigerator for 30 minutes.

6. Preheat oven to 400°F.

7. Drop by rounded tablespoonfuls (or pipe small mounds using a piping bag) about 2 inches apart onto a parchment paper-lined baking sheet.

8. Bake for 20 minutes, then reduce the heat to 375°F and bake for an additional 15-20 minutes until the puffs are golden brown and do not collapse when removed from the oven. These should be uniformly golden all over with no pale sides, and they should sound hollow when tapped. Cool completely on a wire rack.

BLUEBERRY FOOL FILLING

1. Beat the whipping cream, icing sugar, and vanilla extract to firm peaks.

2. Drop the jam by tablespoonfuls over the surface of the whipped cream. Using a rubber spatula, gently fold the jam into the cream. Do not fully blend the two together. You want streaks of jam in the cream if possible.

3. Place the blueberry fool in a piping bag with a large open tip. The larger the tip the better. Push the tip into the creampuff shell and fill the entire inside of the shell with the blueberry fool. If you do not have a piping bag, you can also split the creampuff shells in half with a serrated knife, then spoon the filling into the top and bottom halves before putting them back together.

4. Serve with a dusting of powdered sugar if you like.

Index

A

Apple Cinnamon Sticky Buns, 190
Asian Spice Brined Roast Chicken, 122
Aunt Aggies Peanut Butter Cookies, 210

B

Bacon Fennel Risotto with Seared Scallops, 82
Baked General Tso Chicken, 22
Baked Parmesan Panko Pork Chops with Quick Puttanesca Sauce, 46
Balsamic and Honey Roasted Beets, 152
Barbecue Chicken Chili, 20
Best Apple Pie (Noah's "Just an Apple Pie"), The, 270
Best Bolognese Sauce, The, 50
BLT Salad with Creamy Dijon Dressing and Garlic Herb Butter Croutons, 154
Blueberry Apple Upside-Down Cake, 278
Blueberry Buckle, 174
Blueberry Fool Creampuffs, 282
Blueberry Lemon Cheesecake Bars, 218
Blueberry Lemon Cornmeal Pancakes, 184
Braised Beef Pot Pie with Biscuit Topping, 116
Braised Short-Rib Beef Barley Soup, 142
Brandied Peach Shortcake, 248
British Custard Tart, 260
Brown Butter Cookies, 220
Brown Sugar Pecan Glazed Pork Loin, 124
Burgundy Thyme Pot Roast, 128

C

Carrot Cake Cheesecake, 274
Cherry Muffins with Graham Crumb Streusel, 178
Cherry Orange Pork Medallions, 100
Cherry Pecan Cake, 236
Chicken Carrot and Lentil Soup, 166
Chicken Fried Cod Nuggets with Lime Chive Mayo, 68
Chicken Fried Pork Chops, 52
Chicken Margherita Cannelloni, 28
Chocolate Cherry Upside-Down Cake, 268
Chocolate Walnut Butter Tart Bars, 212
Chorizo Rotisserie Chicken Noodle Soup, 146
Classic Victoria Sandwich Cake, 228
Coconut Shortbread Blueberry Crumble Bars, 222

Creamy Lemon Pepper Scallops Linguine, 88
Crispy Baked Orange Hoisin Chicken, 26
Curry Chicken Burgers with Quick Mango
        Chutney, 30
Curry Pork Chops with Easy Plum Chutney, 40

D

Dijon Beef and Mushroom Pie, 136
Double Chocolate Truffle Cake, 250

E

Easy Five-Spice Ginger Beef, 86
Easy Lemon Dijon Roasted Chicken, 134
Easy Mango Chicken Curry, 18

F

Foolproof Dry-Rubbed Oven Ribs, 130
Frozen Peanut Butter Cup Pie, 276

G

Garlic and Five-Spice Grilled Steak, 54
Garlic Parmesan Potato Latkes, 194
Glazed Sesame Chicken, 16
Gluten Free Chocolate Pavlova Cookies, 204

H

Ham, Sweet Potato, and Spinach Soup, 144
Homemade Jam Jams, 216
Honey Barbecue Pulled Beef Sandwiches with
        Creamy Dijon Coleslaw, 132
Honey Dijon Garlic Chicken Breasts, 10
Honey Roasted Carrots with Mint, 160
Hummingbird Cake, 232

I

Italian Sausage and Chicken Cassoulet, 114

L

Lamingtons, 208
Lemon Herb Roasted Potato Nuggets, 140
Lemon Shrimp Pasta Salad, 148
Lemon Velvet Cake, 230
Low-Fat Chicken Taco Salad with Mango Salsa, 98
Low-Fat Ranch Chicken Salad, 94
Low-Fat Turkey Sausage and Brown Rice, 104

M

Mango Peach Coconut Crumble, 262
Manhattan Style Roasted Vegetable Chorizo Seafood
        Chowder, 64
Meatloaf with Sweet Onion Glaze, 42
Mediterranean Lemon Butter Chicken, 92
Mediterranean Lemon Chicken Orzo Salad, 102
Mini Black Forest Cheesecakes, 256
Moroccan Meatball Stew, 120
Mussels Marinara, 66

N

Newfoundland Dressing (Summer Savoury
        Stuffing), 168
Newfoundland Figgy Duff, 158
Newfoundland Fish Cakes, 62
Newfoundland Raisin Tea Buns, 172
Nutella Swirl Brownies, 224

O

Oatmeal Apple Banana Muffins, 186
Old-Fashioned Lemon Icebox Pie, 266
One Bowl Gingerbread Cake with Mango Vanilla
    Jam, 234
Orange Five-Spice Broiled Chicken, 32
Orange Mint Grilled Shrimp, 108
Oreo Caramel Brownie Bombs, 214
Oven-Fried Chicken Wings with Honey Molasses
    BBQ Sauce, 14

P

Pan-Seared Pork Chops with Dijon Butter
    Sauce, 48
Parmesan Bacon Chicken Linguine, 110
Parmesan Panko Crusted Rack of Lamb, 58
Peanut Butter Sriracha Bacon Cheeseburger, 44
Perfect Cherry Cobbler, 254
Perfect Hot Cross Buns, 182
Perfect Pecan Pie, 258
Popcorn Shrimp with Chili Lime Dipping
    Sauce, 72
Prosciutto Wrapped Roasted Red Pepper
    and Mozzarella Stuffed Chicken Breasts, 34

Q

Quidi Vidi Beer Battered Shrimp with Chili Lime or
    Lime Curry Mayo, 78

R

Raspberry Filled Donut Muffins, 196
Roasted Tomato Fennel Lobster Bisque, 70
Rum Raisin Ice Cream, 264

S

Sage Thyme Chicken Stew with Cornbread
    Dumplings, 126
Salisbury Steak with Mushroom Gravy, 38
Salmon in Pastry with Dijon Cream Sauce, 74
Sausage and Garlic Quiche with Smoked Cheddar
    Sauce, 192
Seafood Shells and Cheese, 76
Smoked Chicken, Spinach, Grilled Pineapple, and
    Pomegranate Salad, 96
Smoked Paprika Chicken and Potatoes, 12

Smoky Chipotle Fried Chicken, 24
Sour Cream Lemon Scones, 188
Souvlaki Roast Pork Loin with Lemon Oregano
    Tzatziki, 56
Spice Velvet Cake, 242
Spicy Ginger Orange Noodles, 164
Spinach Pesto Pappardelle, 150
Sticky Toffee Banana Cake with Cream Cheese
    Frosting, 238
Strawberry Crumble (or Crumble Bars), 206
Strawberry Muffles, 180
Sunken Grape Almond Cake, 176

T

Tarragon and Chive Pan-Fried Cod with Fettuccine
    Puttanesca, 80
Thirty Minute Easy Chicken and Chickpea Curry,
    90
Toasted Coconut Shortbread Cookies, 202
Tomato Fennel Braised Chicken Thighs, 118
Too Tall Neapolitan Cake, 244
Turtle Cookies, 200

U

Ultimate Strawberries and Cream Cake, The, 240

W

Warm Grilled Potato Salad with Lemon and
    Oregano, 156
Warm Roasted Spaghetti Squash and Quinoa Salad,
    162
White Bean Chicken Chili, 106
White Chocolate Cheesecake with Raspberries, 280

Acknowledgements

I remember driving out over Pitts Memorial Drive here in St. John's last Fall for a trade show where I was having my first ever book signing and wondering if anyone would actually come. But come they did, and with such warm and generous spirits. I met several people for the first time with whom I had only interacted online, but strangers we were not. At every book signing, you could tell a *RockRecipes.com* follower by the way they approached the table—always smiling and often with arms outstretched.

Throughout the past year, I have been humbled numerous times by the kindness and support people have shown for my first cookbook. In introducing book two, it is really most important for me to acknowledge all those who provided such great support and encouragement over the past year. Thanks to all of you who bought the book, recommended it to friends, or gave it as a gift. Thanks too for the thousands of messages of support over social media and messages on *RockRecipes.com*. I have read each and every one of them and am so very grateful for them all.

Thanks to my recipe testers, including all my blog readers who give such great feedback on my recipes. Your responses often help to simplify and clarify instructions in my recipes, which benefits all those who use them.

Thanks so much to the terrific crew at Breakwater Books for their great belief that I could write a cookbook in the first place and that it would actually sell! Particular thanks to James Langer for his patience and guidance in editing my books and to Rhonda Molloy for her gorgeous design work that received so many compliments from the buyers of my first cookbook.

Thanks, as always, to Lynn, a.k.a. "Spouse." There is no counting the number of hours of help she has given toward the writing of this book. From shopping to cleaning dishes to prepping the ingredients to holding a photo reflector at just the right angle, she does more than she will ever get proper credit for, but she does it anyway.

Finally, thanks again to the two people I most love to bring to the dinner table, my kids, Olivia and Noah, who always remind me that a family dinner really is worth the effort.

One wife, two kids, one mortgage, lifelong food obsessive, recipe blogger, and food photographer: that's how *Rock Recipes* creator Barry C. Parsons describes himself on his popular food blog, *RockRecipes.com*. Called "one of the best food blogs in Canada" by the *National Post*, *Rock Recipes* boasts over 500,000 followers at home and in the USA. Parsons lives in St. John's, Newfoundland.

Find more from Barry at www.RockRecipes.com

 /RockRecipes   @RockRecipes   /RockRecipes